WITHDRAWN

English Men of Letters

EDITED BY JOHN MORLEY

HAWTHORNE

HAWTHORNE

BY

HENRY JAMES

AMS PRESS
NEW YORK

Reprinted from the edition of 1887, London
First AMS EDITION published 1968
Manufactured in the United States of America

Library of Congress Catalogue Card Number: 68-58383

AMS PRESS, INC.
New York, N.Y. 10003

CONTENTS.

CONTENTS.

CHAPTER V.

CHAPTER VI.

CHAPTER VII.

HAWTHORNE

HAWTHORNE.

CHAPTER I.

EARLY YEARS.

It will be necessary, for several reasons, to give this short sketch the form rather of a critical essay than of a biography. The data for a life of Nathaniel Hawthorne are the reverse of copious, and even if they were abundant they would serve but in a limited measure the purpose of the biographer. Hawthorne's career was probably as tranquil and uneventful a one as ever fell to the lot of a man of letters; it was almost strikingly deficient in incident, in what may be called the dramatic quality. Few men of equal genius and of equal eminence can have led on the whole a simpler life. His six volumes of Note-Books illustrate this simplicity; they are a sort of monument to an unagitated fortune. Hawthorne's career had few vicissitudes or variations; it was passed for the most part in a small and homogeneous society, in a provincial, rural community; it had few perceptible points of contact with what is called the world, with public events, with the manners of his

B

time, even with the life of his neighbours. Its literary
incidents are not numerous. He produced, in quantity,
but little. His works consist of four novels and the
fragment of another, five volumes of short tales, a
collection of sketches, and a couple of story-books for
children. And yet some account of the man and the
writer is well worth giving. Whatever may have been
Hawthorne's private lot, he has the importance of being
the most beautiful and most eminent representative of
a literature. The importance of the literature may be
questioned, but at any rate, in the field of letters,
Hawthorne is the most valuable example of the American genius. That genius has not, as a whole, been
literary; but Hawthorne was on his limited scale a
master of expression. He is the writer to whom his
countrymen most confidently point when they wish to
make a claim to have enriched the mother-tongue, and,
judging from present appearances, he will long occupy
this honourable position. If there is something very
fortunate for him in the way that he borrows an added
relief from the absence of competitors in his own line
and from the general flatness of the literary field that
surrounds him, there is also, to a spectator, something
almost touching in his situation. He was so modest
and delicate a genius that we may fancy him appealing
from the lonely honour of a representative attitude—
perceiving a painful incongruity between his imponder-
able literary baggage and the large conditions of
American life. Hawthorne on the one side is so subtle
and slender and unpretending, and the American world
on the other is so vast and various and substantial, that
it might seem to the author of *The Scarlet Letter* and
the *Mosses from an Old Manse*, that we render him a

poor service in contrasting his proportions with those
of a great civilization. But our author must accept
the awkward as well as the graceful side of his fame;
for he has the advantage of pointing a valuable moral.
This moral is that the flower of art blooms only where
the soil is deep, that it takes a great deal of history to
produce a little literature, that it needs a complex
social machinery to set a writer in motion. American
civilization has hitherto had other things to do than to
produce flowers, and before giving birth to writers it
has wisely occupied itself with providing something for
them to write about. Three or four beautiful talents
of trans-Atlantic growth are the sum of what the world
usually recognises, and in this modest nosegay the
genius of Hawthorne is admitted to have the rarest and
sweetest fragrance.

His very simplicity has been in his favour; it has
helped him to appear complete and homogeneous. To
talk of his being national would be to force the
note and make a mistake of proportion; but he is, in
spite of the absence of the realistic quality, intensely
and vividly local. Out of the soil of New England he
sprang—in a crevice of that immitigable granite he
sprouted and bloomed. Half of the interest that he
possesses for an American reader with any turn for
analysis must reside in his latent New England savour;
and I think it no more than just to say that whatever
entertainment he may yield to those who know him at
a distance, it is an almost indispensable condition of
properly appreciating him to have received a personal
impression of the manners, the morals, indeed of the
very climate, of the great region of which the remarkable city of Boston is the metropolis. The cold, bright

air of New England seems to blow through his pages, and these, in the opinion of many people, are the medium in which it is most agreeable to make the acquaintance of that tonic atmosphere. As to whether it is worth while to seek to know something of New England in order to extract a more intimate quality from *The House of Seven Gables* and *The Blithedale Romance*, I need not pronounce; but it is certain that a considerable observation of the society to which these productions were more directly addressed is a capital preparation for enjoying them. I have alluded to the absence in Hawthorne of that quality of realism which is now so much in fashion, an absence in regard to which there will of course be more to say; and yet I think I am not fanciful in saying that he testifies to the sentiments of the society in which he flourished almost as pertinently (proportions observed) as Balzac and some of his descendants—MM. Flaubert and Zola—testify to the manners and morals of the French people. He was not a man with a literary theory; he was guiltless of a system, and I am not sure that he had ever heard of Realism, this remarkable compound having (although it was invented some time earlier) come into general use only since his death. He had certainly not proposed to himself to give an account of the social idiosyncrasies of his fellow-citizens, for his touch on such points is always light and vague, he has none of the apparatus of an historian, and his shadowy style of portraiture never suggests a rigid standard of accuracy. Nevertheless he virtually offers the most vivid reflection of New England life that has found its way into literature. His value in this respect is not diminished by the fact that he has not attempted

to portray the usual Yankee of comedy, and that he
has been almost culpably indifferent to his opportunities
for commemorating the variations of colloquial English
that may be observed in the New World. His characters
do not express themselves in the dialect of the *Biglow
Papers*—their language indeed is apt to be too elegant,
too delicate. They are not portraits of actual types,
and in their phraseology there is nothing imitative.
But none the less, Hawthorne's work savours thoroughly
of the local soil—it is redolent of the social system in
which he had his being.

This could hardly fail to be case, when the man
himself was so deeply rooted in the soil. Hawthorne
sprang from the primitive New England stock ; he had a
very definite and conspicuous pedigree. He was born at
Salem, Massachusetts, on the 4th of July, 1804, and his
birthday was the great American festival, the anniversary of the Declaration of national Independence.[1]
Hawthorne was in his disposition an unqualified and
unflinching American ; he found occasion to give us the
measure of the fact during the seven years that he spent
in Europe toward the close of his life ; and this was no
more than proper on the part of a man who had enjoyed

[1] It is proper that before I go further I should acknowledge my
large obligations to the only biography of our author, of any considerable length, that has been written—the little volume entitled
A Study of Hawthorne, by Mr. George Parsons Lathrop, the son-
in-law of the subject of the work. (Boston, 1876.) To this ingenious and sympathetic sketch, in which the author has taken
great pains to collect the more interesting facts of Hawthorne's
life, I am greatly indebted. Mr. Lathrop's work is not pitched
in the key which many another writer would have chosen, and his
tone is not to my sense the truly critical one ; but without the
help afforded by his elaborate essay, the present little volume could
not have been prepared.

the honour of coming into the world on the day on
which of all the days in the year the great Republic
enjoys her acutest fit of self-consciousness.   Moreover,
a person who has been ushered into life by the ringing
of bells and the booming of cannon (unless indeed he be
frightened straight out of it again by the uproar of his
awakening) receives by this very fact an injunction to
do something great, something that will justify such
striking natal accompaniments.   Hawthorne was by
race of the clearest Puritan strain.   His earliest
American ancestors (who wrote the name " Hathorne "
—the shape in which it was transmitted to Nathaniel,
who inserted the *w*,) was the younger son of a Wiltshire
family, whose residence, according to a note of our
author's in 1837, was " Wigcastle, Wigton."   Hawthorne, in the note in question, mentions the gentleman who was at that time the head of the family ;
but it does not appear that he at any period renewed
acquaintance with his English kinsfolk.   Major William
Hathorne came out to Massachusetts in the early years
of the Puritan settlement ; in 1635 or 1636, according
to the note to which I have just alluded ; in 1630 according to information presumably more accurate.   He
was one of the band of companions of the virtuous and
exemplary John Winthrop, the almost lifelong royal
Governor of the young colony, and the brightest and
most amiable figure in the early Puritan annals.
How amiable William Hathorne may have been I
know not, but he was evidently of the stuff of which
the citizens of the Commonwealth were best advised to
be made.   He was a sturdy fighting man, doing solid
execution upon both the inward and outward enemies
of the State.   The latter were the savages, the former

the Quakers; the energy expended by the early Puritans
in resistance to the tomahawk not weakening their disposition to deal with spiritual dangers.   They employed
the same—or almost the same—weapons in both direc-
tions; the flintlock and the halberd against the Indians,
and the cat-o'-nine-tails against the heretics.   One of
the longest, though by no means one of the most successful, of Hawthorne's shorter tales (*The Gentle Boy*)
deals with this pitiful persecution of the least aggressive
of all schismatic bodies.   William Hathorne, who had
been made a magistrate of the town of Salem, where a
grant of land had been offered him as an inducement to
residence, figures in New England history as having
given orders that "Anne Coleman and four of her
friends" should be whipped through Salem, Boston,
and Dedham.   This Anne Coleman, I suppose, is the
woman alluded to in that fine passage in the Introduction to *The Scarlet Letter*, in which Hawthorne pays
a qualified tribute to the founder of the American branch
of his race :—

"The figure of that first ancestor, invested by family
tradition with a dim and dusky grandeur, was present to my
boyish imagination as far back as I can remember.   It still
haunts me, and induces a sort of home-feeling with the past,
which I scarcely claim in reference to the present, phase of
the town.   I seem to have a stronger claim to a residence
here on account of this grave, bearded, sable-cloaked and
steeple-crowned progenitor—who came so early, with his Bible
and his sword, and trod the unworn street with such a stately
port, and make so large a figure as a man of war and peace—
a stronger claim than for myself, whose name is seldom
heard and my face hardly known.   He was a soldier, legis-
lator, judge; he was a ruler in the church; he had all the
Puritanic traits, both good and evil.   He was likewise a bitter

persecutor, as witness the Quakers, who have remembered
him in their histories, and relate an incident of his hard
severity towards a woman of their sect which will last
longer, it is to be feared, than any of his better deeds, though
these were many."

William Hathorne died in 1681 ; but those hard
qualities that his descendant speaks of were reproduced
in his son John, who bore the title of Colonel, and who
was connected, too intimately for his honour, with that
deplorable episode of New England history, the persecution of the so-called Witches of Salem. John Hathorne
is introduced into the little drama entitled *The Salem
Farms* in Longfellow's *New England Tragedies*. I
know not whether he had the compensating merits of
his father, but our author speaks of him, in the con-
tinuation of the passage I have just quoted, as having
made himself so conspicuous in the martyrdom of the
witches, that their blood may be said to have left a
stain upon him. " So deep a stain, indeed," Hawthorne
adds, characteristically, " that his old dry bones in
the Charter Street burial-ground must still retain it,
if they have not crumbled utterly to dust." Readers
of *The House of the Seven Gables* will remember that the
story concerns itself with a family which is supposed to
be overshadowed by a curse launched against one of its
earlier members by a poor man occupying a lowlier place
in the world, whom this ill-advised ancestor had been
the means of bringing to justice for the crime of witch-
craft. Hawthorne apparently found the idea of the
history of the Pyncheons in his own family annals.
His witch-judging ancestor was reported to have
incurred a malediction from one of his victims, in
consequence of which the prosperity of the race faded

utterly away. "I know not," the passage I have
already quoted goes on, "whether these ancestors of
mine bethought themselves to repent and ask pardon
of Heaven for their cruelties, or whether they are
now groaning under the heavy consequences of them
in another state of being. At all events, I, the present
writer, hereby take shame upon myself for their sakes,
and pray that any curse incurred by them—as I have
heard, and as the dreary and unprosperous condition
of the race for some time back would argue to exist—
may be now and henceforth removed." The two first
American Hathornes had been people of importance
and responsibility; but with the third generation the
family lapsed into an obscurity from which it emerged
in the very person of the writer who begs so gracefully
for a turn in its affairs. It is very true, Hawthorne
proceeds, in the Introduction to *The Scarlet Letter*,
that from the original point of view such lustre as he
might have contrived to confer upon the name would
have appeared more than questionable.

" Either of these stern and black-browed Puritans would
have thought it quite a sufficient retribution for his sins that
after so long a lapse of years the old trunk of the family
tree, with so much venerable moss upon it, should have borne,
as its topmost bough, an idler like myself. No aim that I
have ever cherished would they recognise as laudable; no
success of mine, if my life, beyond its domestic scope, had
ever been brightened by success, would they deem otherwise
than worthless, if not positively disgraceful. ' What is he ? '
murmurs one grey shadow of my forefathers to the other.
' A writer of story-books ! What kind of a business in life,
what manner of glorifying God, or being serviceable to
mankind in his day and generation, may that be ? Why, the
degenerate fellow might as well have been a fiddler ! ' Such

are the compliments bandied between my great grandsires and myself across the gulf of time! And yet, let them scorn me as they will, strong traits of their nature have intertwined themselves with mine."

In this last observation we may imagine that there was not a little truth. Poet and novelist as Hawthorne was, sceptic and dreamer and little of a man of action, late-coming fruit of a tree which might seem to have lost the power to bloom, he was morally, in an appreciative degree, a chip of the old block. His forefathers had crossed the Atlantic for conscience' sake, and it was the idea of the urgent conscience that haunted the imagination of their so-called degenerate successor. The Puritan strain in his blood ran clear—there are passages in his Diaries, kept during his residence in Europe, which might almost have been written by the grimmest of the old Salem worthies. To him as to them, the consciousness of *sin* was the most importunate fact of life, and if they had undertaken to write little tales, this baleful substantive, with its attendant adjective, could hardly have been more frequent in their pages than in those of their fanciful descendant. Hawthorne had moreover in his composition, contemplator and dreamer as he was, an element of simplicity and rigidity, a something plain and masculine and sensible, which might have kept his black-browed grandsires on better terms with him than he admits to be possible. However little they might have appreciated the artist, they would have approved of the man. The play of Hawthorne's intellect was light and capricious, but the man himself was firm and rational. The imagination was profane, but the temper was not degenerate.

The " dreary and unprosperous condition " that he

speaks of in regard to the fortunes of his family is an allusion to the fact that several generations followed each other on the soil in which they had been planted, that during the eighteenth century a succession of Hathornes trod the simple streets of Salem without ever conferring any especial lustre upon the town or receiving, presumably, any great delight from it. A hundred years of Salem would perhaps be rather a dead-weight for any family to carry, and we venture to imagine that the Hathornes were dull and depressed. They did what they could, however, to improve their situation; they trod the Salem streets as little as possible. They went to sea, and made long voyages; seamanship became the regular profession of the family. Hawthorne has said it in charming language. "From father to son, for above a hundred years, they followed the sea; a grey-headed shipmaster, in each generation, retiring from the quarter-deck to the homestead, while a boy of fourteen took the hereditary place before the mast, confronting the salt spray and the gale which had blustered against his sire and grandsire. The boy also, in due time, passed from the forecastle to the cabin, spent a tempestuous manhood, and returned from his world-wanderings to grow old and die and mingle his dust with the natal earth." Our author's grandfather, Daniel Hathorne, is mentioned by Mr. Lathrop, his biographer and son-in-law, as a hardy privateer during the war of Independence. His father, from whom he was named, was also a shipmaster, and he died in foreign lands, in the exercise of his profession. He was carried off by a fever, at Surinam, in 1808. He left three children, of whom Nathaniel was the only boy. The boy's mother, who had been a Miss Manning, came of a New England stock almost as long-established as that of her husband; she is described by our author's biographer as a woman of remarkable beauty, and by an authority whom he quotes, as being "a minute observer of religious festivals," of "feasts, fasts, new-moons, and Sabbaths." Of feasts the poor lady in her Puritanic home can have had but a very limited number to celebrate; but of new-moons, she may be supposed to have enjoyed the usual, and of Sabbaths even more than the usual, proportion.

In quiet provincial Salem, Nathaniel Hawthorne passed the greater part of his boyhood, as well as many years of his later life. Mr. Lathrop has much to say about the ancient picturesqueness of the place, and about the mystic influences it would project upon such a mind and character as Hawthorne's. These things are always relative, and in appreciating them everything depends upon the point of view. Mr. Lathrop writes for American readers, who in such a matter as this are very easy to please. Americans have as a general thing a hungry passion for the picturesque, and they are so fond of local colour that they contrive to perceive it in localities in which the amateurs of other countries would detect only the most neutral tints. History, as yet, has left in the United States but so thin and impalpable a deposit that we very soon touch the hard substratum of nature; and nature herself, in the western world, has the peculiarity of seeming rather crude and immature. The very air looks new and young; the light of the sun seems fresh and innocent, as if it knew as yet but few of the secrets of the world and none of the weariness of shining; the vegetation has the appearance of not having reached its

majority. A large juvenility is stamped upon the face
of things, and in the vividness of the present, the past,
which died so young and had time to produce so little,
attracts but scanty attention. I doubt whether English
observers would discover any very striking trace of it
in the ancient town of Salem. Still, with all respect
to a York and a Shrewsbury, to a Toledo and a Verona,
Salem has a physiognomy in which the past plays a
more important part than the present. It is of course
a very recent past; but one must remember that the
dead of yesterday are not more alive than those of a
century ago. I know not of what picturesqueness
Hawthorne was conscious in his respectable birthplace ;
I suspect his perception of it was less keen than his
biographer assumes it to have been ; but he must have
felt at least that of whatever complexity of earliér life
there had been in the country, the elm-shadowed streets
of Salem were a recognisable memento. He has made
considerable mention of the place, here and there, in
his tales ; but he has nowhere dilated upon it very
lovingly, and it is noteworthy that in *The House of the
Seven Gables*, the only one of his novels of which the
scene is laid in it, he has by no means availed himself
of the opportunity to give a description of it. He had
of course a filial fondness for it—a deep-seated sense
of connection with it ; but he must have spent some
very dreary years there, and the two feelings, the
mingled tenderness and rancour, are visible in the
Introduction to *The Scarlet Letter*.

" The old town of Salem," he writes,—" my native place,
though I have dwelt much away from it, both in boyhood and
in maturer years—possesses, or did possess, a hold on my
affections, the force of which I have never realized during my

seasons of actual residence here. Indeed, so far as the physical aspect is concerned, with its flat, unvaried surface, covered chiefly with wooden houses, few or none of which pretend to architectural beauty; its irregularity, which is neither picturesque nor quaint, but only tame ; its long and lazy street, lounging wearisomely through the whole extent of the peninsula, with Gallows Hill and New Guinea at one end, and a view of the almshouse at the other—such being the features of my native town it would be quite as reasonable to form a sentimental attachment to a disarranged chequer-board."

But he goes on to say that he has never divested himself of the sense of intensely belonging to it—that the spell of the continuity of his life with that of his predecessors has never been broken. "It is no matter that the place is joyless for him; that he is weary of the old wooden houses, the mud and the dust, the dead level of site and sentiment, the chill east wind, and the chilliest of social atmospheres;—all these and whatever faults besides he may see or imagine, are nothing to the purpose. The spell survives, and just as powerfully as if the natal spot were an earthly paradise." There is a very American quality in this perpetual consciousness of a spell on Hawthorne's part; it is only in a country where newness and change and brevity of tenure are the common substance of life, that the fact of one's ancestors having lived for a hundred and seventy years in a single spot would become an element of one's morality. It is only an imaginative American that would feel urged to keep reverting to this circumstance, to keep analysing and cunningly considering it.

The Salem of to-day has, as New England towns go, a physiognomy of its own, and in spite of Hawthorne's analogy of the disarranged draught-board, it is a

decidedly agreeable one.   The spreading elms in its
streets, the proportion of large, square, honourable-look-
ing houses, suggesting an easy, copious material life, the
little gardens, the grassy waysides, the open windows,
the air of space and salubrity and decency, and above
all the intimation of larger antecedents—these things
compose a picture which has little of the element that
painters call depth of tone, but which is not without
something that they would admit to be style.   To
English eyes the oldest and most honourable of the
smaller American towns must seem in a manner primitive and rustic ; the shabby, straggling, village-quality
appears marked in them, and their social tone is not
unnaturally inferred to bear the village stamp.   Village-
like they are, and it would be no gross incivility to
describe them as large, respectable, prosperous, democratic villages.   But even a village, in a great and
vigorous democracy, where there are no overshadowing
squires, where the " county " has no social existence,
where the villagers are conscious of no superincumbent
strata of gentility, piled upwards into vague regions of
privilege—even a village is not an institution to accept
of more or less graceful patronage ; it thinks extremely
well of itself, and is absolute in its own regard.   Salem
is a sea-port, but it is a sea-port deserted and decayed.
It belongs to that rather melancholy group of old coast-
towns, scattered along the great sea-face of New England,
and of which the list is completed by the names of
Portsmouth, Plymouth, New Bedford, Newburyport,
Newport—superannuated centres of the traffic with
foreign lands, which have seen their trade carried away
from them by the greater cities.   As Hawthorne says,
their ventures have gone " to swell, needlessly and

imperceptibly, the mighty flood of commerce at New York or Boston." Salem, at the beginning of the present century, played a great part in the Eastern trade; it was the residence of enterprising shipowners who despatched their vessels to Indian and Chinese seas. It was a place of large fortunes, many of which have remained, though the activity that produced them has passed away. These successful traders constituted what Hawthorne calls "the aristocratic class." He alludes in one of his slighter sketches (*The Sister Years*) to the sway of this class and the "moral influence of wealth" having been more marked in Salem than in any other New England town. The sway, we may believe, was on the whole gently exercised, and the moral influence of wealth was not exerted in the cause of immorality. Hawthorne was probably but imperfectly conscious of an advantage which familiarity had made stale—the fact that he lived in the most democratic and most virtuous of modern communities. Of the virtue it is but civil to suppose that his own family had a liberal share; but not much of the wealth, apparently, came into their way. Hawthorne was not born to a patrimony, and his income, later in life, never exceeded very modest proportions.

Of his childish years there appears to be nothing very definite to relate, though his biographer devotes a good many graceful pages to them. There is a considerable sameness in the behaviour of small boys, and it is probable that if we were acquainted with the details of our author's infantine career we should find it to be made up of the same pleasures and pains as that of many ingenuous lads for whom fame has had nothing in keeping.

The absence of precocious symptoms of genius is on
the whole more striking in the lives of men who have
distinguished themselves than their juvenile promise;
though it must be added that Mr. Lathrop has made
out, as he was almost in duty bound to do, a very good
case in favour of Hawthorne's having been an interesting child. He was not at any time what would be
called a sociable man, and there is therefore nothing
unexpected in the fact that he was fond of long walks
in which he was not known to have had a companion.
"Juvenile literature" was but scantily known at that
time, and the enormous and extraordinary contribution
made by the United States to this department of human
happiness was locked in the bosom of futurity. The
young Hawthorne, therefore, like many of his con-
temporaries, was constrained to amuse himself, for want
of anything better, with the *Pilgrim's Progress* and the
Faery Queen. A boy may have worse company than
Bunyan and Spenser, and it is very probable that in
his childish rambles our author may have had associates
of whom there could be no record. When he was nine
years old he met with an accident at school which
threatened for a while to have serious results. He was
struck on the foot by a ball and so severely lamed that
he was kept at home for a long time, and had not completely recovered before his twelfth year. His school,
it is to be supposed, was the common day-school of New
England—the primary factor in that extraordinarily
pervasive system of instruction in the plainer branches
of learning, which forms one of the principal ornaments
of American life. In 1818, when he was fourteen years
old, he was taken by his mother to live in the house of
an uncle, her brother, who was established in the town

C

of Raymond, near Lake Sebago, in the State of Maine.
The immense State of Maine, in the year 1818, must
have had an even more magnificently natural character
than it possesses at the present day, and the uncle's
dwelling, in consequence of being in a little smarter
style than the primitive structures that surrounded it,
was known by the villagers as Manning's Folly. Mr.
Lathrop pronounces this region to be of a "weird and
woodsy" character; and Hawthorne, later in life, spoke
of it to a friend as the place where "I first got my
cursed habits of solitude." The outlook, indeed, for an
embryonic novelist, would not seem to have been cheerful; the social dreariness of a small New England community lost amid the forests of Maine, at the beginning
of the present century, must have been consummate.
But for a boy with a relish for solitude there were many
natural resources, and we can understand that Hawthorne should in after years have spoken very tenderly
of this episode. "I lived in Maine like a bird of the
air, so perfect was the freedom I enjoyed." During the
long summer days he roamed, gun in hand, through
the great woods, and during the moonlight nights of
winter, says his biographer, quoting another informant,
"he would skate until midnight, all alone, upon Sebago
Lake, with the deep shadows of the icy hills on either
hand."

In 1819 he was sent back to Salem to school, and in
the following year he wrote to his mother, who had remained at Raymond (the boy had found a home at Salem
with another uncle), "I have left school and have begun
to fit for college under Benjm. L. Oliver, Lawyer. So
you are in danger of having one learned man in your
family. . . . I get my lessons at home and recite them

to him (Mr. Oliver) at seven o'clock in the morning. . .
. . Shall you want me to be a Minister, Doctor, or
Lawyer? A Minister I will not be." He adds, at the
close of this epistle—" O how I wish I was again with
you, with nothing to do but to go a-gunning ! But the
happiest days of my life are gone." In 1821, in his
seventeenth year, he entered Bowdoin College, at Bruns-
wick, Maine. This institution was in the year 1821—a
quarter of a century after its foundation—a highly
honourable, but not a very elaborately organized, nor
a particularly impressive, seat of learning. I say it
was not impressive, but I immediately remember that
impressions depend upon the minds receiving them ; and
that to a group of simple New England lads, upwards of
sixty years ago, the halls and groves of Bowdoin, neither
dense nor lofty though they can have been, may have
seemed replete with Academic stateliness. It was a
homely, simple, frugal, " country college," of the old-
fashioned American stamp ; exerting within its limits
a civilizing influence, working, amid the forests and
the lakes, the log-houses and the clearings, toward the
amenities and humanities and other collegiate graces,
and offering a very sufficient education to the future
lawyers, merchants, clergymen, politicians, and editors,
of the very active and knowledge-loving community
that supported it. It did more than this—it numbered
poets and statesmen among its undergraduates, and on
the roll-call of its sons it has several distinguished
names. Among Hawthorne's fellow-students was Henry
Wadsworth Longfellow, who divides with our author
the honour of being the most distinguished of American
men of letters. I know not whether Mr. Longfellow
was especially intimate with Hawthorne at this period

(they were very good friends later in life), but with two
of his companions he formed a friendship which lasted
always.   One of these was Franklin Pierce, who was
destined to fill what Hawthorne calls " the most august
position in the world."   Pierce was elected President of
the United States in 1852.   The other was Horatio
Bridge, who afterwards served with distinction in the
Navy, and to whom the charming prefatory letter of
the collection of tales published under the name of *The
Snow Image*, is addressed.   " If anybody is responsible
at this day for my being an author it is yourself.   I
know not whence your faith came; but while we were
lads together at a country college—gathering blueberries in study-hours under those tall Academic pines ;
or watching the great logs as they tumbled along the
current of the Androscoggin ; or shooting pigeons and
grey squirrels in the woods; or bat-fowling in the
summer twilight ; or catching trout in that shadowy
little stream which, I suppose, is still wandering river-
ward through the forest—though you and I will never
cast a line in it again—two idle lads, in short (as we
need not fear to acknowledge now), doing a hundred
things the Faculty never heard of, or else it had been
worse for us—still it was your prognostic of your friend's
destiny that he was, to be a writer of fiction."   That is
a very pretty picture, but it is a picture of happy urchins
at school, rather than of undergraduates " panting," as
Macaulay says, " for one and twenty."   Poor Hawthorne
was indeed thousands of miles away from Oxford and
Cambridge; that touch about the blueberries and the
logs on the Androscoggin tells the whole story, and
strikes the note, as it were, of his circumstances.   But
if the pleasures at Bowdoin were not expensive, so

neither were the penalties. The amount of Hawthorne's
collegiate bill for one term was less than 4*l*., and of
this sum more than 9*s*. was made up of fines. The
fines, however, were not heavy. Mr. Lathrop prints a
letter addressed by the President to " Mrs. Elizabeth C.
Hathorne," requesting her co-operation with the officers
of this college, " in the attempt to induce your son
faithfully to observe the laws of this institution." He
has just been fined fifty cents for playing cards for money
during the preceding term. " Perhaps he might not
have gamed," the Professor adds, " were it not for the
influence of a student whom we have dismissed from
college." The biographer quotes a letter from Hawthorne to one of his sisters, in which the writer says, in
allusion to this remark, that it is a great mistake to
think that he has been led away by the wicked ones. " I
was fully as willing to play as the person he suspects
of having enticed me, and would have been influenced
by no one. I have a great mind to commence playing
again, merely to show him that I scorn to be seduced
by another into anything wrong." There is something
in these few words that accords with the impression
that the observant reader of Hawthorne gathers of the
personal character that underlay his duskily-sportive
imagination—an impression of simple manliness and
transparent honesty.

He appears to have been a fair scholar, but not a
brilliant one ; and it is very probable that as the standard of scholarship at Bowdoin was not high, he graduated none the less comfortably on this acccunt. Mr.
Lathrop is able to testify to the fact, by no means a
surprising one, that he wrote verses at college, though
the few stanzas that the biographer quotes are not

such as to make us especially regret that his rhyming
mood was a transient one.

> " The ocean hath its silent caves,
>   Deep, quiet and alone.
>   Though there be fury on the waves,
>   Beneath them there is none."

That quatrain may suffice to decorate our page. And
in connection with his college days I may mention his
first novel, a short romance entitled *Fanshawe*, which
was published in Boston in 1828, three years after he
graduated. It was probably also written after that
event, but the scene of the tale is laid at Bowdoin
(which figures under an altered name), and Hawthorne's attitude with regard to the book, even shortly
after it was published, was such as to assign it to
this boyish period. It was issued anonymously, but
he so repented of his venture that he annihilated the
edition, of which, according to Mr. Lathrop, "not
half a dozen copies are now known to be extant." I
have seen none of these rare volumes, and I know
nothing of *Fanshawe* but what the writer just quoted
relates. It is the story of a young lady who goes in
rather an odd fashion to reside at " Harley College"
(equivalent of Bowdoin), under the care and guardian-
ship of Dr. Melmoth, the President of the institution,
a venerable, amiable, unworldly, and henpecked scholar.
Here she becomes very naturally an object of interest
to two of the students ; in regard to whom I cannot do
better than quote Mr. Lathrop. One of these young men
" is Edward Wolcott, a wealthy, handsome, generous,
healthy young fellow from one of the seaport towns ;
and the other Fanshawe, the hero, who is a poor
but ambitious recluse, already passing into a decline

through overmuch devotion to books and meditation.
Fanshawe, though the deeper nature of the two, and
intensely moved by his new passion, perceiving that a
union between himself and Ellen could not be a happy
one, resigns the hope of it from the beginning. But circumstances bring him into intimate relation with her.
The real action of the book, after the preliminaries,
takes up only some three days, and turns upon the
attempt of a man named Butler to entice Ellen away
under his protection, then marry her, and secure the
fortune to which she is heiress. This scheme is partly
frustrated by circumstances, and Butler's purpose
towards Ellen thus becomes a much more sinister one.
From this she is rescued by Fanshawe, and knowing
that he loves her, but is concealing his passion, she
gives him the opportunity and the right to claim her
hand. For a moment the rush of desire and hope is
so great that he hesitates; then he refuses to take
advantage of her generosity, and parts with her for a
last time. Ellen becomes engaged to Wolcott, who had
won her heart from the first; and Fanshawe, sinking
into rapid consumption, dies before his class graduates."
The story must have had a good deal of innocent lightness; and it is a proof of how little the world of observation lay open to Hawthorne, at this time, that he
should have had no other choice than to make his
little drama go forward between the rather naked walls
of Bowdoin, where the presence of his heroine was
an essential incongruity. He was twenty-four years
old, but the "world," in its social sense, had not disclosed itself to him. He had, however, already, at
moments, a very pretty writer's touch, as witness this
passage, quoted by Mr. Lathrop, and which is worth

transcribing. The heroine has gone off with the nefarious Butler, and the good Dr. Melmoth starts in pursuit of her, attended by young Wolcott.

" ' Alas, youth, these are strange times,' observed the President, ' when a doctor of divinity and an undergraduate set forth, like a knight-errant and his squire, in search of a stray damsel. Methinks I am an epitome of the church militant, or a new species of polemical divinity. Pray Heaven, however, there be no such encounter in store for us ; for I utterly forgot to provide myself with weapons.'

" ' I took some thought for that matter, reverend knight,' replied Edward, whose imagination was highly tickled by Dr. Melmoth's chivalrous comparison.

" ' Aye, I see that you have girded on a sword,' said the divine. ' But wherewith shall I defend myself ? my hand being empty except of this golden-headed staff, the gift of Mr. Langton.'

" ' One of these, if you will accept it,' answered Edward, exhibiting a brace of pistols, ' will serve to begin the conflict before you join the battle hand to hand.'

" ' Nay, I shall find little safety in meddling with that deadly instrument, since I know not accurately from which end proceeds the bullet,' said Dr. Melmoth. ' But were it not better, since we are so well provided with artillery, to betake ourselves, in the event of an encounter, to some stone wall or other place of strength ?

" ' If I may presume to advise,' said the squire, ' you, as being most valiant and experienced, should ride forward, lance in hand (your long staff serving for a lance), while I annoy the enemy from afar.'

" ' Like Teucer, behind the shield of Ajax,' interrupted Dr. Melmoth, ' or David with his stone and sling. No, no, young man ; I have left unfinished in my study a learned treatise, important not only to the present age, but to posterity, for whose sake I must take heed to my safety. But, lo ! who rides yonder ? ' "

On leaving college Hawthorne had gone back to live at Salem.

CHAPTER II.

THE twelve years that followed were not the happiest or most brilliant phase of Hawthorne's life; they strike me indeed as having had an altogether peculiar dreariness. They had their uses; they were the period of incubation of the admirable compositions which eventually brought him reputation and prosperity. But of their actual aridity the young man must have had a painful consciousness; he never lost the impression of it. Mr. Lathrop quotes a phrase to this effect from one of his letters, late in life. " I am disposed to thank God for the gloom and chill of my early life, in the hope that my share of adversity came then, when I bore it alone." And the same writer alludes to a touching passage in the English Note-Books, which I shall quote entire :—

" I think I have been happier this Christmas (1854) than ever before—by my own fireside, and with my wife and children about me—more content to enjoy what I have, less anxious for anything beyond it, in this life. My early life was perhaps a good preparation for the declining half of life; it having been such a blank that any thereafter would compare favourably with it. For a long, long while, I have occasionally

been visited with a singular dream; and I have an impression
that I have dreamed it ever since I have been in England. It
is, that I am still at college, or, sometimes, even, at school—
and there is a sense that I have been there unconscionably
long, and have quite failed to make such progress as my con-
temporaries have done; and I seem to meet some of them
with a feeling of shame and depression that broods over me
as I think of it, even when awake. This dream, recurring all
through these twenty or thirty years, must be one of the
effects of that heavy seclusion in which I shut myself up for
twelve years after leaving college, when everybody moved
onward and left me behind. How strange that it should
come now, when I may call myself famous and prosperous!
—when I am happy too."

The allusion here is to a state of solitude which was
the young man's positive choice at the time—or into
which he drifted at least under the pressure of his
natural shyness and reserve. He was not expansive,
he was not addicted to experiments and adventures of
intercourse, he was not, personally, in a word, what
is called sociable. The general impression of this
silence-loving and shade-seeking side of his character
is doubtless exaggerated, and, in so far as it points to
him as a sombre and sinister figure, is almost ludicrously
at fault. He was silent, diffident, more inclined to hesi-
tate, to watch and wait and meditate, than to produce
himself, and fonder, on almost any occasion, of being
absent than of being present. This quality betrays itself
in all his writings. There is in all of them something
cold and light and thin, something belonging to the
imagination alone, which indicates a man but little
disposed to multiply his relations, his points of contact,
with society. If we read the six volumes of Note-
Books with an eye to the evidence of this unsocial side

of his life, we find it in sufficient abundance. But we find at the same time that there was nothing unamiable or invidious in his shyness, and above all that there was nothing preponderantly gloomy. The qualities to which the Note-Books most testify are, on the whole, his serenity and amenity of mind. They reveal these characteristics indeed in an almost phenomenal degree. The serenity, the simplicity, seem in certain portions almost child-like; of brilliant gaiety, of high spirits, there is little; but the placidity and evenness of temper, the cheerful and contented view of the things he notes, never belie themselves. I know not what else he may have written in this copious record, and what passages of gloom and melancholy may have been suppressed ; but as his Diaries stand, they offer in a remarkable degree the reflection of a mind whose development was not in the direction of sadness. A very clever French critic, whose fancy is often more lively than his observation is deep, M. Emile Montégut, writing in the *Revue des Deux Mondes,* in the year 1860, invents for our author the appellation of " Un Romancier Pessimiste." Superficially speaking, perhaps, the title is a happy one ; but only superficially. Pessimism consists in having morbid and bitter views and theories about human nature ; not in indulging in shadowy fancies and conceits. There is nothing whatever to show that Hawthorne had any such doctrines or convictions ; certainly, the note of depression, of despair, of the disposition to undervalue the human race, is never sounded in his Diaries. These volumes contain the record of very few convictions or theories of any kind ; they move with curious evenness, with a charming, graceful flow, on a level which lies above that of a man's

philosophy. They adhere with such persistence to this
upper level that they prompt the reader to believe that
Hawthorne had no appreciable philosophy at all—no
general views that were in the least uncomfortable.
They are the exhibition of an unperplexed intellect.   I
said just now that the development of Hawthorne's
mind was not towards sadness ; and I should be inclined to go still further, and say that his mind proper—
his mind in so far as it was a repository of opinions and
articles of faith—had no development that it is of especial
importance to look into.   What had a development was
his imagination—that delicate and penetrating imagination which was always at play, always entertaining
itself, always engaged in a game of hide and seek in
the region in which it seemed to him that the game
could best be played—among the shadows and sub-
structions, the dark-based pillars and supports, of our
moral nature.   Beneath this movement and ripple of
his imagination—as free and spontaneous as that of the
sea surface—lay directly his personal affections.   These
were solid and strong, but, according to my impression,
they had the place very much to themselves.

His innocent reserve, then, and his exaggerated, but
by no means cynical, relish for solitude, imposed themselves upon him, in a great measure, with a persistency
which helped to make the time a tolerably arid one—so
arid a one indeed that we have seen that in the light of
later happiness he pronounced it a blank.   But in truth,
if these were dull years, it was not all Hawthorne's
fault.   His situation was intrinsically poor—poor with
a poverty that one almost hesitates to look into.   When
we think of what the conditions of intellectual life, of
taste, must have been in a small New England town

fifty years ago; and when we think of a young man of
beautiful genius, with a love of literature and romance,
of the picturesque, of style and form and colour, trying
to make a career for himself in the midst of them, compassion for the young man becomes our dominant sentiment, and we see the large dry village picture in perhaps
almost too hard a light. It seems to me then that it
was possibly a blessing for Hawthorne that he was not
expansive and inquisitive, that he lived much to himself
and asked but little of his *milieu*. If he had been
exacting and ambitious, if his appetite had been large
and his knowledge various, he would probably have
found the bounds of Salem intolerably narrow. But
his culture had been of a simple sort—there was little
of any other sort to be obtained in America in those
days, and though he was doubtless haunted by visions
of more suggestive opportunities, we may safely assume
that he was not to his own perception the object of
compassion that he appears to a critic who judges him
after half a century's civilization has filtered into the
twilight of that earlier time. If New England was
socially a very small place in those days, Salem was a
still smaller one; and if the American tone at large
was intensely provincial, that of New England was
not greatly helped by having the best of it. The state
of things was extremely natural, and there could be
now no greater mistake than to speak of it with a
redundancy of irony. American life had begun to constitute itself from the foundations; it had begun to *be*,
simply; it was at an immeasurable distance from having
begun to enjoy. I imagine there was no appreciable
group of people in New England at that time proposing
to itself to enjoy life; this was not an undertaking for

which any provision had been made, or to which any encouragement was offered. Hawthorne must have vaguely entertained some such design upon destiny; but he must have felt that his success would have to depend wholly upon his own ingenuity. I say he must have proposed to himself to enjoy, simply because he proposed to be an artist, and because this enters inevitably into the artist's scheme. There are a thousand ways of enjoying life, and that of the artist is one of the most innocent. But for all that, it connects itself with the idea of pleasure. He proposes to give pleasure, and to give it he must first get it. Where he gets it will depend upon circumstances, and circumstances were not encouraging to Hawthorne.

He was poor, he was solitary, and he undertook to devote himself to literature in a community in which the interest in literature was as yet of the smallest. It is not too much to say that even to the present day it is a considerable discomfort in the United States not to be " in business." The young man who attempts to launch himself in a career that does not belong to the so-called practical order; the young man who has not, in a word, an office in the business-quarter of the town, with his name painted on the door, has but a limited place in the social system, finds no particular bough to perch upon. He is not looked at askance, he is not regarded as an idler; literature and the arts have always been held in extreme honour in the American world, and those who practise them are received on easier terms than in other countries. If the tone of the American world is in some respects provincial, it is in none more so than in this matter of the exaggerated homage rendered to authorship. The gentleman or the

lady who has written a book is in many circles the
object of an admiration too indiscriminating to operate
as an encouragement to good writing.   There is no
reason to suppose that this was less the case fifty years
ago ; but fifty years ago, greatly more than now, the
literary man must have lacked the comfort and inspiration of belonging to a class.   The best things come, as
a general thing, from the talents that are members of a
group ; every man works better when he has companions
working in the same line, and yielding the stimulus of
suggestion, comparison, emulation.   Great things of
course have been done by solitary workers; but they
have usually been done with double the pains they
would have cost if they had been produced in more
genial circumstances.   The solitary worker loses the
profit of example and discussion ; he is apt to make
awkward experiments ; he is in the nature of the case
more or less of an empiric.   The empiric may, as I say,
be treated by the world as an expert ; but the drawbacks and discomforts of empiricism remain to him,
and are in fact increased by the suspicion that is mingled with his gratitude, of a want in the public taste of
a sense of the proportions of things.   Poor Hawthorne,
beginning to write subtle short tales at Salem, was
empirical enough ; he was one of, at most, some dozen
Americans who had taken up literature as a profession.
The profession in the United States is still very young,
and of diminutive stature ; but in the year 1830 its
head could hardly have been seen above ground.   It
strikes the observer of to-day that Hawthorne showed
great courage in entering a field in which the honours
and emoluments were so scanty as the profits of authorship must have been at that time.   I have said that in

the United States at present authorship is a pedestal,
and literature is the fashion; but Hawthorne's history
is a proof that it was possible, fifty years ago, to write
a great many little masterpieces without becoming
known.   He begins the preface to the *Twice-Told Tales*
by remarking that he was " for many years the obscurest
man of letters in America." When once this work
obtained recognition, the recognition left little to be
desired.   Hawthorne never, I believe, made large sums
of money by his writings, and the early profits of these
charming sketches could not have been considerable;
for many of them, indeed, as they appeared in journals
and magazines, he had never been paid at all; but
the honour, when once it dawned—and it dawned
tolerably early in the author's career—was never thereafter wanting.   Hawthorne's countrymen are solidly
proud of him, and the tone of Mr. Lathrop's *Study* is
in itself sufficient evidence of the manner in which an
American story-teller may in some cases look to have
his eulogy pronounced.

Hawthorne's early attempt to support himself by his
pen appears to have been deliberate; we hear nothing
of those experiments in counting-houses or lawyers'
offices, of which a permanent invocation to the Muse is
often the inconsequent sequel.   He began to write, and
to try and dispose of his writings; and he remained at
Salem apparently only because his family, his mother
and his two sisters, lived there.   His mother had a
house, of which during the twelve years that elapsed
until 1838, he appears to have been an inmate.   Mr.
Lathrop learned from his surviving sister that after
publishing *Fanshawe* he produced a group of short
stories entitled *Seven Tales of my Native Land*, and that

this lady retained a very favourable recollection of the
work, which her brother had given her to read.   But
it never saw the light; his attempts to get it published
were unsuccessful, and at last, in a fit of irritation and
despair, the young author burned the manuscript.

There is probably something autobiographic in the
striking little tale of *The Devil in Manuscript*.   " They
have been offered to seventeen publishers," says the
hero of that sketch in regard to a pile of his own
lucubrations.

"It would make you stare to read their answers. . . . .
One man publishes nothing but school-books; another has
five novels already under examination ; . . . . another gentleman is just giving up business, on purpose, I verily believe,
to avoid publishing my book.   In short, of all the seventeen
booksellers, only one has vouchsafed even to read my tales ;
and he—a literary dabbler himself, I should judge—has the
impertinence to criticise them, proposing what he calls vast
improvements, and concluding, after a general sentence of
condemnation, with the definitive assurance that he will not
be concerned on any terms. . . . . But there does seem to be
one righteous man among these seventeen unrighteous ones,
and he tells me, fairly, that no American publisher will
meddle with an American work — seldom if by a known
writer, and never if by a new one—unless at the writer's
risk."

But though the *Seven Tales* were not printed, Hawthorne proceeded to write others that were; the two
collections of the *Twice-Told Tales*, and the *Snow Image*,
are gathered from a series of contributions to the local
journals and the annuals of that day.   To make these
three volumes, he picked out the things he thought the
best.   "Some very small part," he says of what remains, "might yet be rummaged out (but it would not

D

be worth the trouble), among the dingy pages of fifteen or twenty-years-old periodicals, or within the shabby morocco covers of faded *Souvenirs*." These three volumes represent no large amount of literary labour for so long a period, and the author admits that there is little to show "for the thought and industry of that portion of his life." He attributes the paucity of his productions to a "total lack of sympathy at the age when his mind would naturally have been most effervescent." "He had no incitement to literary effort in a reasonable prospect of reputation or profit; nothing but the pleasure itself of composition, an enjoyment not at all amiss in its way, and perhaps essential to the merit of the work in hand, but which in the long run will hardly keep the chill out of a writer's heart, or the numbness out of his fingers." These words occur in the preface attached in 1851 to the second edition of the *Twice-Told Tales ; à propos* of which I may say that there is always a charm in Hawthorne's prefaces which makes one grateful for a pretext to quote from them. At this time *The Scarlet Letter* had just made his fame, and the short tales were certain of a large welcome; but the account he gives of the failure of the earlier edition to produce a sensation (it had been published in two volumes, at four years apart), may appear to contradict my assertion that, though he was not recognised immediately, he was recognised betimes. In 1850, when *The Scarlet Letter* appeared, Hawthorne was forty-six years old, and this may certainly seem a long-delayed popularity. On the other hand, it must be remembered that he had not appealed to the world with any great energy. The *Twice-Told Tales*, charming as they are, do not constitute a very massive literary pedestal. As soon as the author, resorting to severer measures, put forth *The Scarlet Letter*, the public ear was touched and charmed, and after that it was held to the end. " Well it might have been ! " the reader will exclaim. " But what a grievous pity that the dulness of this same organ should have operated so long as a deterrent, and by making Hawthorne wait till he was nearly fifty to publish his first novel, have abbreviated by so much his productive career ! " The truth is, he cannot have been in any very high degree ambitious ; he was not an abundant producer, and there was manifestly a strain of generous indolence in his composition. There was a loveable want of eagerness about him. Let the encouragement offered have been what it might, he had waited till he was lapsing from middle-life to strike his first noticeable blow ; and during the last ten years of his career he put forth but two complete works, and the fragment of a third.

It is very true, however, that during this early period he seems to have been very glad to do whatever came to his hand. Certain of his tales found their way into one of the annuals of the time, a publication endowed with the brilliant title of *The Boston Token and Atlantic Souvenir*. The editor of this graceful repository was S. G. Goodrich, a gentleman who, I suppose, may be called one of the pioneers of American periodical literature. He is better known to the world as Mr. Peter Parley, a name under which he produced a multitude of popular school-books, story-books, and other attempts to vulgarize human knowledge and adapt it to the infant mind. This enterprising purveyor of literary wares appears, incongruously enough, to have been Hawthorne's earliest protector, if protection is

D 2

the proper word for the treatment that the young
author received from him. Mr. Goodrich induced him
in 1836 to go to Boston to edit a periodical in which he
was interested, *The American Magazine of Useful and
Entertaining Knowledge.* I have never seen the work
in question, but Hawthorne's biographer gives a sorry
account of it. It was managed by the so-called Bewick
Company, which "took its name from Thomas Bewick,
the English restorer of the art of wood-engraving, and
the magazine was to do his memory honour by his admirable illustrations. But in fact it never did any one
honour, nor brought any one profit. It was a penny
popular affair, containing condensed information about
innumerable subjects, no fiction, and little poetry.
The woodcuts were of the crudest and most frightful
sort. It passed through the hands of several editors
and several publishers. Hawthorne was engaged at a
salary of five hundred dollars a year; but it appears
that he got next to nothing, and did not stay in the
position long." Hawthorne wrote from Boston in the
winter of 1836: "I came here trusting to Goodrich's
positive promise to pay me forty-five dollars as soon as
I arrived; and he has kept promising from one day to
another, till I do not see that he means to pay at all.
I have now broke off all intercourse with him, and
never think of going near him. . . . . I don't feel
at all obliged to him about the editorship, for he is a
stockholder and director in the Bewick Company . . . .
and I defy them to get another to do for a thousand
dollars, what I do for five hundred."—"I make nothing,"
he says in another letter, "of writing a history or
biography before dinner." Goodrich proposed to him
to write a *Universal History* for the use of schools,

offering him a hundred dollars for his share in the work.
Hawthorne accepted the offer and took a hand—I know
not how large a one—in the job. His biographer has
been able to identify a single phrase as our author's.
He is speaking of George IV : " Even when he was
quite a young man this King cared as much about dress
as any young coxcomb. He had a great deal of taste
in such matters, and it is a pity that he was a King, for
he might otherwise have made an excellent tailor."
The *Universal History* had a great vogue and passed
through hundreds of editions; but it does not appear
that Hawthorne ever received more than his hundred
dollars. The writer of these pages vividly remembers
making its acquaintance at an early stage of his education—a very fat, stumpy-looking book, bound in boards
covered with green paper, and having in the text very
small woodcuts, of the most primitive sort. He
associates it to this day with the names of Sesostris
and Semiramis whenever he encounters them, there
having been, he supposes, some account of the conquests
of these potentates that would impress itself upon the
imagination of a child. At the end of four months,
Hawthorne had received but twenty dollars—four
pounds—for his editorship of the *American Magazine*.

There is something pitiful in this episode, and something really touching in the sight of a delicate and
superior genius obliged to concern himself with such
paltry undertakings. The simple fact was that for a
man attempting at that time in America to live by his
pen, there were no larger openings ; and to live at all
Hawthorne had, as the phrase is, to make himself small.
This cost him less, moreover, than it would have cost
a more copious and strenuous genius, for his modesty

was evidently extreme, and I doubt whether he had any very ardent consciousness of rare talent. He went back to Salem, and from this tranquil standpoint, in the spring of 1837, he watched the first volume of his *Twice-Told Tales* come into the world. He had by this time been living some ten years of his manhood in Salem, and an American commentator may be excused for feeling the desire to construct, from the very scanty material that offers itself, a slight picture of his life there. I have quoted his own allusions to its dulness and blankness, but I confess that these observations serve rather to quicken than to depress my curiosity. A biographer has of necessity a relish for detail; his business is to multiply points of characterisation. Mr. Lathrop tells us that our author " had little communication with even the members of his family. Frequently his meals were brought and left at his locked door, and it was not often that the four inmates of the old Herbert Street mansion met in family circle. He never read his stories aloud to his mother and sisters. . . It was the custom in this household for the several members to remain very much by themselves; the three ladies were perhaps nearly as rigorous recluses as himself, and, speaking of the isolation which reigned among them, Hawthorne once said, ' We do not even *live* at our house ! ' " It is added that he was not in the habit of going to church. This is not a lively picture, nor is that other sketch of his daily habits much more exhilarating, in which Mr. Lathrop affirms that though the statement that for several years " he never saw the sun " is entirely an error, yet it is true that he stirred little abroad all day and " seldom chose to walk in the town except at night." In the dusky hours he took walks of many miles along the

coast, or else wandered about the sleeping streets of
Salem. These were his pastimes, and these were apparently his most intimate occasions of contact with
life. Life, on such occasions, was not very exuberant,
as any one will reflect who has been acquainted with
the physiognomy of a small New England town after
nine o'clock in the evening. Hawthorne, however, was
an inveterate observer of small things, and he found a
field for fancy among the most trivial accidents. There
could be no better example of this happy faculty than the
little paper entitled "Night Sketches," included among
the *Twice-Told Tales*. This small dissertation is about
nothing at all, and to call attention to it is almost to
overrate its importance. This fact is equally true,
indeed, of a great many of its companions, which give
even the most appreciative critic a singular feeling of
his own indiscretion—almost of his own cruelty. They
are so light, so slight, so tenderly trivial, that simply
to mention them is to put them in a false position. The
author's claim for them is barely audible, even to the
most acute listener. They are things to take or to
leave—to enjoy, but not to talk about. Not to read
them would be to do them an injustice (to read them is
essentially to relish them), but to bring the machinery
of criticism to bear upon them would be to do them a
still greater wrong. I must remember, however, that
to carry this principle too far would be to endanger the
general validity of the present little work—a consum-
mation which it can only be my desire to avert. Therefore it is that I think it permissible to remark that
in Hawthorne, the whole class of little descriptive
effusions directed upon common things, to which these
just-mentioned Night Sketches belong, have a greater

charm than there is any warrant for in their substance. The charm is made up of the spontaneity, the personal quality, of the fancy that plays through them, its mingled simplicity and subtlety, its purity and its *bonhomie*. The Night Sketches are simply the light, familiar record of a walk under an umbrella, at the end of a long, dull, rainy day, through the sloppy, ill-paved streets of a country town, where the rare gas-lamps twinkle in the large puddles, and the blue jars in the druggist's window shine through the vulgar drizzle. One would say that the inspiration of such a theme could have had no great force, and such doubtless was the case ; but out of the Salem puddles, nevertheless, springs, flower-like, a charming and natural piece of prose.

I have said that Hawthorne was an observer of small things, and indeed he appears to have thought nothing too trivial to be suggestive. His Note-Books give us the measure of his perception of common and casual things, and of his habit of converting them into *memoranda*. These Note-Books, by the way—this seems as good a place as any other to say it—are a very singular series of volumes; I doubt whether there is anything exactly corresponding to them in the whole body of literature. They were published— in six volumes, issued at intervals—some years after Hawthorne's death, and no person attempting to write an account of the romancer could afford to regret that they should have been given to the world. There is a point of view from which this may be regretted ; but the attitude of the biographer is to desire as many documents as possible. I am thankful, then, as a biographer, for the Note-Books, but I am obliged to

confess that, though I have just re-read them carefully,
I am still at a loss to perceive how they came to be
written—what was Hawthorne's purpose in carrying on
for so many years this minute and often trivial chronicle.
For a person desiring information about him at any
cost, it is valuable; it sheds a vivid light upon his
character, his habits, the nature of his mind. But we
find ourselves wondering what was its value to Hawthorne himself. It is in a very partial degree a register
of impressions, and in a still smaller sense a record of
emotions. Outward objects play much the larger part
in it; opinions, convictions, ideas pure and simple, are
almost absent. He rarely takes his Note-Book into his
confidence or commits to its pages any reflections that
might be adapted for publicity; the simplest way to
describe the tone of these extremely objective journals
is to say that they read like a series of very pleasant,
though rather dullish and decidedly formal, letters,
addressed to himself by a man who, having suspicions
that they might be opened in the post, should have
determined to insert nothing compromising. They contain much that is too futile for things intended for publicity; whereas, on the other hand, as a receptacle of
private impressions and opinions, they are curiously cold
and empty. They widen, as I have said, our glimpse of
Hawthorne's mind (I do not say that they elevate our
estimate of it), but they do so by what they fail to contain, as much as by what we find in them. Our business
for the moment, however, is not with the light that they
throw upon his intellect, but with the information they
offer about his habits and his social circumstances.

I know not at what age he began to keep a diary;
the first entries in the American volumes are of the

summer of 1835. There is a phrase in the preface to
his novel of *Transformation*, which must have lingered
in the minds of many Americans who have tried to
write novels and to lay the scene of them in the
western world. " No author, without a trial, can
conceive of the difficulty of writing a romance about
a country where there is no shadow, no antiquity, no
mystery, no picturesque and gloomy wrong, nor anything but a commonplace prosperity, in broad and
simple daylight, as is happily the case with my dear
native land." The perusal of Hawthorne's American
Note-Books operates as a practical commentary upon this
somewhat ominous text. It does so at least to my own
mind; it would be too much perhaps to say that the
effect would be the same for the usual English reader.
An American reads between the lines—he completes the
suggestions—he constructs a picture. I think I am not
guilty of any gross injustice in saying that the picture
he constructs from Hawthorne's American diaries,
though by no means without charms of its own, is
not, on the whole, an interesting one. It is characterised by an extraordinary blankness—a curious paleness
of colour and paucity of detail. Hawthorne, as I have
said, has a large and healthy appetite for detail, and one
is therefore the more struck with the lightness of the diet
to which his observation was condemned. For myself,
as I turn the pages of his journals, I seem to see the
image of the crude and simple society in which he lived.
I use these epithets, of course, not invidiously, but de-
scriptively; if one desire to enter as closely as possible
into Hawthorne's situation, one must endeavour to re-
produce his circumstances. We are struck with the
large number of elements that were absent from them,

and the coldness, the thinness, the blankness, to repeat
my epithet, present themselves so vividly that our fore-
most feeling is that of compassion for a romancer looking
for subjects in such a field. It takes so many things, as
Hawthorne must have felt later in life, when he made
the acquaintance of the denser, richer, warmer European
spectacle—it takes such an accumulation of history and
custom, such a complexity of manners and types, to form
a fund of suggestion for a novelist. If Hawthorne had
been a young Englishman, or a young Frenchman of the
same degree of genius, the same cast of mind, the same
habits, his consciousness of the world around him would
have been a very different affair; however obscure, however reserved, his own personal life, his sense of the life
of his fellow-mortals would have been almost infinitely
more various. The negative side of the spectacle on
which Hawthorne looked out, in his contemplative
saunterings and reveries, might, indeed, with a little
ingenuity, be made almost ludicrous; one might enume-
rate the items of high civilization, as it exists in other
countries, which are absent from the texture of American life, until it should become a wonder to know what
was left. No State, in the European sense of the word, and
indeed barely a specific national name. No sovereign, no
court, no personal loyalty, no aristocracy, no church, no
clergy, no army, no diplomatic service, no country gentle-
men, no palaces, no castles, nor manors, nor old country-
houses, nor parsonages, nor thatched cottages nor ivied
ruins; no cathedrals, nor abbeys, nor little Norman
churches; no great Universities nor public schools—no
Oxford, nor Eton, nor Harrow; no literature, no novels,
no museums, no pictures, no political society, no sporting
class—no Epsom nor Ascot! Some such list as that

might be drawn up of the absent things in American life
—especially in the American life of forty years ago, the
effect of which, upon an English or a French imagination, would probably as a general thing be appalling.
The natural remark, in the almost lurid light of such an
indictment, would be that if these things are left out,
everything is left out. The American knows that a good
deal remains; what it is that remains — that is his
secret, his joke, as one may say. It would be cruel, in
this terrible denudation, to deny him the consolation of
his national gift, that "American humour" of which
of late years we have heard so much.

But in helping us to measure what remains, our
author's Diaries, as I have already intimated, would give
comfort rather to persons who might have taken the
alarm from the brief sketch I have just attempted of
what I have called the negative side of the American
social situation, than to those reminding themselves of
its fine compensations. Hawthorne's entries are to a
great degree accounts of walks in the country, drives
in stage-coaches, people he met in taverns. The minute-
ness of the things that attract his attention and that he
deems worthy of being commemorated is frequently
extreme, and from this fact we get the impression of
a general vacancy in the field of vision. "Sunday
evening, going by the jail, the setting sun kindled up
the windows most cheerfully ; as if there were a bright,
comfortable light within its darksome stone wall." "I
went yesterday with Monsieur S——— to pick rasp-
berries. He fell through an old log-bridge, thrown over
a hollow ; looking back, only his head and shoulders
appeared through the rotten logs and among the
bushes.—A shower coming on, the rapid running of a

little barefooted boy, coming up unheard, and dashing
swiftly past us, and showing us the soles of his naked
feet as he ran adown the path and up the opposite side."
In another place he devotes a page to a description of a
dog whom he saw running round after its tail ; in still
another he remarks, in a paragraph by itself—"The
aromatic odor of peat-smoke, in the sunny autumnal
air is very pleasant."   The reader says to himself that
when a man turned thirty gives a place in his mind—
and his inkstand—to such trifles as these, it is because
nothing else of superior importance demands admission.
Everything in the Notes indicates a simple, democratic,
thinly-composed society ; there is no evidence of the
writer finding himself in any variety or intimacy of
relations with any one or with anything.   We find a
good deal of warrant for believing that if we add that
statement of Mr. Lathrop's about his meals being left
at the door of his room, to rural rambles of which an
impression of the temporary phases of the local apple-
crop were the usual, and an encounter with an organ-
grinder, or an eccentric dog, the rarer, outcome, we
construct a rough image of our author's daily life
during the several years that preceded his marriage.
He appears to have read a good deal, and that he must
have been familiar with the sources of good English we
see from his charming, expressive, slightly self-conscious,
cultivated, but not too cultivated, style.   Yet neither in
these early volumes of his Note-Books, nor in the later,
is there any mention of his reading.   There are no
literary judgments or impressions—there is almost no
allusion to works or to authors.   The allusions to individuals of any kind are indeed much less numerous
than one might have expected ; there is little psychology,

little description of manners. We are told by
Mr. Lathrop that there existed at Salem during the
early part of Hawthorne's life "a strong circle of
wealthy families," which "maintained rigorously the
distinctions of class," and whose "entertainments were
splendid, their manners magnificent." This is a rather
pictorial way of saying that there were a number of
people in the place—the commercial and professional
aristocracy, as it were—who lived in high comfort and
respectability, and who, in their small provincial way,
doubtless had pretensions to be exclusive. Into this
delectable company Mr. Lathrop intimates that his hero
was free to penetrate. It is easy to believe it, and it
would be difficult to perceive why the privilege should
have been denied to a young man of genius and culture,
who was very good-looking (Hawthorne must have been
in these days, judging by his appearance later in life, a
strikingly handsome fellow), and whose American pedigree was virtually as long as the longest they could
show. But in fact Hawthorne appears to have ignored
the good society of his native place almost completely; no echo of its conversation is to be found in
his tales or his journals. Such an echo would possibly
not have been especially melodious, and if we regret the
shyness and stiffness, the reserve, the timidity, the suspicion, or whatever it was, that kept him from knowing
what there was to be known, it is not because we have
any very definite assurance that his gains would have
been great. Still, since a beautiful writer was growing
up in Salem, it is a pity that he should not have given
himself a chance to commemorate some of the types that
flourished in the richest soil of the place. Like almost
all people who possess in a strong degree the story·

telling faculty, Hawthorne had a democratic strain in
his composition and a relish for the commoner stuff of
human nature.   Thoroughly American in all ways, he
was in none more so than in the vagueness of his sense
of social distinctions and his readiness to forget them if
a moral or intellectual sensation were to be gained by it.
He liked to fraternise with plain people, to take them
on their own terms, and put himself if possible into their
shoes.   His Note-Books, and even his tales, are full of
evidence of this easy and natural feeling about all his
unconventional fellow-mortals—this imaginative interest
and contemplative curiosity—and it sometimes takes the
most charming and graceful forms.   Commingled as it
is with his own subtlety and delicacy, his complete
exemption from vulgarity, it is one of the points in his
character which his reader comes most to appreciate—
that reader I mean for whom he is not as for some few,
a dusky and malarious genius.

But even if he had had, personally, as many pretensions as he had few, he must in the nature of things
have been more or less of a consenting democrat, for
democracy was the very key-stone of the simple social
structure in which he played his part.   The air of his
journals and his tales alike are full of the genuine
democratic feeling. This feeling has by no means passed
out of New England life ; it still flourishes in perfection
in the great stock of the people, especially in rural
communities ; but it is probable that at the present
hour a writer of Hawthorne's general fastidiousness
would not expresss it quite so artlessly.   "A shrewd
gentlewoman, who kept a tavern in the town," he says,
in *Chippings with a Chisel,* " was anxious to obtain two
or three gravestones for the deceased members of her

family, and to pay for these solemn commodities by
taking the sculptor to board." This image of a
gentlewoman keeping a tavern and looking out for
boarders, seems, from the point of view to which I
allude, not at all incongruous. It will be observed that
the lady in question was shrewd; it was probable that
she was substantially educated, and of reputable life,
and it is certain that she was energetic. These qualities
would make it natural to Hawthorne to speak of her as
a gentlewoman; the natural tendency in societies where
the sense of equality prevails, being to take for granted
the high level rather than the low. Perhaps the most
striking example of the democratic sentiment in all our
author's tales, however, is the figure of Uncle Venner,
in *The House of the Seven Gables.* Uncle Venner is a
poor old man in a brimless hat and patched trousers,
who picks up a precarious subsistence by rendering, for
a compensation, in the houses and gardens of the good
people of Salem, those services that are know in New
England as "chores." He carries parcels, splits fire-
wood, digs potatoes, collects refuse for the maintenance of
his pigs, and looks forward with philosophic equanimity
to the time when he shall end his days in the almshouse.
But in spite of the very modest place that he occupies in
the social scale, he is received on a footing of familiarity
in the household of the far-descended Miss Pyncheon;
and when this ancient lady and her companions take the
air in the garden of a summer evening, he steps into the
estimable circle and mingles the smoke of his pipe with
their refined conversation. This obviously is rather
imaginative—Uncle Venner is a creation with a purpose. He is an original, a natural moralist, a philoso-
pher; and Hawthorne, who knew perfectly what he

was about in introducing him—Hawthorne always
knew perfectly what he was about—wished to give in
his person an example of humorous resignation and of
a life reduced to the simplest and homeliest elements, as
opposed to the fantastic pretensions of the antiquated
heroine of the story.   He wished to strike a certain
exclusively human and personal note.   He knew that
for this purpose he was taking a licence ; but the point
is that he felt he was not indulging in any extravagant
violation of reality.   Giving in a letter, about 1830, an
account of a little journey he was making in Connecti-
cut, he says, of the end of a seventeen miles' stage,
that "in the evening, however, I went to a Bible-class
with a very polite and agreeable gentleman, whom I
afterwards discovered to be a strolling tailor of very
questionable habits."

Hawthorne appears on various occasions to have
absented himself from Salem, and to have wandered
somewhat through the New England States.   But the
only one of these episodes of which there is a considerable account in the Note-Books is a visit that he
paid in the summer of 1837 to his old college-mate,
Horatio Bridge, who was living upon his father's property in Maine, in company with an eccentric young
Frenchman, a teacher of his native tongue, who was
looking for pupils among the northern forests.   I have
said that there was less psychology in Hawthorne's
Journals than might have been looked for ; but there
is nevertheless a certain amount of it, and nowhere
more than in a number of pages relating to this remarkable "Monsieur S." (Hawthorne, intimate as he apparently became with him, always calls him "Monsieur,"
just as throughout all his Diaries he invariably speaks

E

of all his friends, even the most familiar, as "Mr."
He confers the prefix upon the unconventional Thoreau,
his fellow-woodsman at Concord, and upon the emancipated brethren at Brook Farm.) These pages are completely occupied with Monsieur S., who was evidently
a man of character, with the full complement of his
national vivacity. There is an elaborate effort to
analyse the poor young Frenchman's disposition, something conscientious and painstaking, respectful, explicit,
almost solemn. These passages are very curious as a
reminder of the absence of the off-hand element in the
manner in which many Americans, and many New
Englanders especially, make up their minds about
people whom they meet. This, in turn, is a reminder
of something that may be called the importance of the
individual in the American world; which is a result
of the newness and youthfulness of society and of
the absence of keen competition. The individual counts
for more, as it were, and, thanks to the absence of a
variety of social types and of settled heads under which
he may be easily and conveniently pigeon-holed, he is to
a certain extent a wonder and a mystery. An Englishman, a Frenchman—a Frenchman above all—judges
quickly, easily, from his own social standpoint, and
makes an end of it. He has not that rather chilly
and isolated sense of moral responsibility which is apt
to visit a New Englander in such processes; and he
has the advantage that his standards are fixed by the
general consent of the society in which he lives. A
Frenchman, in this respect, is particularly happy and
comfortable, happy and comfortable to a degree which I
think is hardly to be over-estimated; his standards
being the most definite in the world, the most easily and

promptly appealed to, and the most identical with what happens to be the practice of the French genius itself. The Englishman is not quite so well off, but he is better off than his poor interrogative and tentative cousin beyond the seas. He is blessed with a healthy mistrust of analysis, and hair-splitting is the occupation he most despises. There is always a little of the Dr. Johnson in him, and Dr. Johnson would have had wofully little patience with that tendency to weigh moonbeams which in Hawthorne was almost as much a quality of race as of genius; albeit that Hawthorne has paid to Boswell's hero (in the chapter on " Lichfield and Uttoxeter," in his volume on England), a tribute of the finest appreciation. American intellectual standards are vague, and Hawthorne's countrymen are apt to hold the scales with a rather uncertain hand and a somewhat agitated conscience.

CHAPTER III.

THE second volume of the *Twice-Told Tales* was published in 1845, in Boston; and at this time a good many
of the stories which were afterwards collected into the
Mosses from an Old Manse had already appeared, chiefly
in *The Democratic Review*, a sufficiently flourishing periodical of that period. In mentioning these things
I anticipate; but I touch upon the year 1845 in order
to speak of the two collections of *Twice-Told Tales* at
once. During the same year Hawthorne edited an
interesting volume, the *Journals of an African Cruiser*,
by his friend Bridge, who had gone into the Navy and
seen something of distant waters. His biographer
mentions that even then Hawthorne's name was thought
to bespeak attention for a book, and he insists on this
fact in contradiction to the idea that his productions
had hitherto been as little noticed as his own declaration that he remained " for a good many years the
obscurest man of letters in America," might lead one,
and has led many people, to suppose   " In this dismal
chamber FAME was won," he writes in Salem in 1836.

And we find in the Note-Books (1840), this singularly beautiful and touching passage :—

" Here I sit in my old accustomed chamber, where I used to sit in days gone by. . . . . Here I have written many tales—many that have been burned to ashes, many that have doubtless deserved the same fate. This claims to be called a haunted chamber, for thousands upon thousands of visions have appeared to me in it ; and some few of them have become visible to the world. If ever I should have a biographer, he ought to make great mention of this chamber in my memoirs, because so much of my lonely youth was wasted here, and here my mind and character were formed ; and here I have been glad and hopeful, and here I have been despondent. And here I sat a long, long time, waiting patiently for the world to know me, and sometimes wondering why it did not know me sooner, or whether it would ever know me at all—at least till I were in my grave. And sometimes it seems to me as if I were already in the grave, with only life enough to be chilled and benumbed. But oftener I was happy—at least as happy as I then knew how to be, or was aware of the possibility of being. By and by the world found me out in my lonely chamber and called me forth—not indeed with a loud roar of acclamation, but rather with a still small voice—and forth I went, but found nothing in the world I thought preferable to my solitude till now. . . . . And now I begin to understand why I was imprisoned so many years in this lonely chamber, and why I could never break through the viewless bolts and bars ; for if I had sooner made my escape into the world, I should have grown hard and rough, and been covered with earthly dust, and my heart might have become callous by rude encounters with the multitude. . . . . But living in solitude till the fulness of time was come, I still kept the dew of my youth and the freshness of my heart. . . . . I used to think that I could imagine all passions, all feelings, and states of the heart and mind ; but how little did I know ! . . . . Indeed, we are but shadows ; we are not endowed with real life, and all that

seems most real about us is but the thinnest substance of a
dream—till the heart be touched. That touch creates us—
then we begin to be—thereby we are beings of reality and
inheritors of eternity."

There is something exquisite in the soft philosophy
of this little retrospect, and it helps us to appreciate it
to know that the writer had at this time just become
engaged to be married to a charming and accomplished
person, with whom his union, which took place two
years later, was complete and full of happiness. But I
quote it more particularly for the evidence it affords
that, already in 1840, Hawthorne could speak of the
world finding him out and calling him forth, as of an
event tolerably well in the past. He had sent the first
of the *Twice-Told* series to his old college friend, Longfellow, who had already laid, solidly, the foundation of
his great poetic reputation, and at the time of his send-
ing it had written him a letter from which it will be
to our purpose to quote a few lines :—

" You tell me you have met with troubles and changes. I
know not what these may have been ; but I can assure you
that trouble is the next best thing to enjoyment, and that
there is no fate in the world so horrible as to have no share
in either its joys or sorrows. For the last ten years I have
not lived, but only dreamed of living. It may be true that
there may have been some unsubstantial pleasures here in the
shade, which I might have missed in the sunshine, but you
cannot conceive how utterly devoid of satisfaction all my
retrospects are. I have laid up no treasure of pleasant
remembrances against old age ; but there is some comfort in
thinking that future years may be more varied, and therefore
more tolerable, than the past. You give me more credit than
I deserve in supposing that I have led a studious life. I have
indeed turned over a good many books, but in so desultory a

way that it cannot be called study, nor has it left me the fruits
of study. . . . . I have another great difficulty in the lack of
materials ; for I have seen so little of the world that I have
nothing but thin air to concoct my stories of, and it is not
easy to give a life-like semblance to such shadowy stuff.
Sometimes, through a peephole, I have caught a glimpse of
the real world, and the two or three articles in which I have
portrayed these glimpses please me better than the others."

It is more particularly for the sake of the concluding
lines that I have quoted this passage ; for evidently no
portrait of Hawthorne at this period is at all exact
which fails to insist upon the constant struggle which
must have gone on between his shyness and his desire
to know something of life ; between what may be called
his evasive and his inquisitive tendencies. I suppose it
is no injustice to Hawthorne to say that on the whole
his shyness always prevailed ; and yet, obviously, the
struggle was constantly there. He says of his *Twice-
Told Tales,* in the preface, " They are not the talk of a
secluded man with his own mind and heart (had it been
so they could hardly have failed to be more deeply and
permanently valuable,) but his attempts, and very imperfectly successful ones, to open an intercourse with
the world." We are speaking here of small things, it
must be remembered—of little attempts, little sketches,
a little world. But everything is relative, and this
smallness of scale must not render less apparent the
interesting character of Hawthorne's efforts. As for
the *Twice-Told Tales* themselves, they are an old story
now ; every one knows them a little, and those who
admire them particularly have read them a great many
times. The writer of this sketch belongs to the latter
class, and he has been trying to forget his familiarity

with them, and ask himself what impression they would
have made upon him at the time they appeared, in the
first bloom of their freshness, and before the particular
Hawthorne-quality, as it may be called, had become an
established, a recognised and valued, fact. Certainly,
I am inclined to think, if one had encountered these
delicate, dusky flowers in the blossomless garden of
American journalism, one would have plucked them
with a very tender hand ; one would have felt that here
was something essentially fresh and new ; here, in no
extraordinary force or abundance, but in a degree distinctly appreciable, was an original element in literature.
When I think of it, I almost envy Hawthorne's earliest
readers ; the sensation of opening upon *The Great Carbuncle, The Seven Vagabonds,* or *The Threefold Destiny* in
an American annual of forty years ago, must have been
highly agreeable.

Among these shorter things (it is better to speak
of the whole collection, including the *Snow Image,*
and the *Mosses from an Old Manse* at once) there
are three sorts of tales, each one of which has an
original stamp. There are, to begin with, the stories of
fantasy and allegory—those among which the three
I have just mentioned would be numbered, and which
on the whole, are the most original. This is the group
to which such little masterpieces as *Malvin's Burial,
Rappacini's Daughter,* and *Young Goodman Brown*
also belong—these two last perhaps representing
the highest point that Hawthorne reached in this
direction. Then there are the little tales of New England history, which are scarcely less admirable, and of
which *The Grey Champion, The Maypole of Merry Mount,*
and the four beautiful *Legends of the Province House,* as

they are called, are the most successful specimens.
Lastly come the slender sketches of actual scenes and
of the objects and manners about him, by means of
which, more particularly, he endeavoured " to open an
intercourse with the world," and which, in spite of their
slenderness, have an infinite grace and charm. Among
these things *A Rill from the Town Pump, The Village
Uncle, The Toll-Gatherer's Day*, the *Chippings with a
Chisel*, may most naturally be mentioned. As we turn
over these volumes we feel that the pieces that spring
most directly from his fancy, constitute, as I have said
(putting his four novels aside), his most substantial
claim to our attention. It would be a mistake to insist
too much upon them; Hawthorne was himself the first
to recognise that. "These fitful sketches," he says in
the preface to the *Mosses from an Old Manse*, "with so
little of external life about them, yet claiming no pro-
fundity of purpose—so reserved even while they sometimes seem so frank—often but half in earnest, and
never, even when most so, expressing satisfactorily the
thoughts which they profess to image—such trifles, I
truly feel, afford no solid basis for a literary reputation."
This is very becomingly uttered; but it may be said,
partly in answer to it, and partly in confirmation, that
the valuable element in these things was not what
Hawthorne put into them consciously, but what passed
into them without his being able to measure it—the
element of simple genius, the quality of imagination.
This is the real charm of Hawthorne's writing—this
purity and spontaneity and naturalness of fancy. For
the rest, it is interesting to see how it borrowed a particular colour from the other faculties that lay near it
—how the imagination, in this capital son of the old

Puritans, reflected the hue of the more purely moral part, of the dusky, overshadowed conscience. The conscience, by no fault of its own, in every genuine offshoot of that sombre lineage, lay under the shadow of the sense of *sin*. This darkening cloud was no essential part of the nature of the individual; it stood fixed in the general moral heaven under which he grew up and looked at life. It projected from above, from outside, a black patch over his spirit, and it was for him to do what he could with the black patch. There were all sorts of possible ways of dealing with it; they depended upon the personal temperament. Some natures would let it lie as it fell, and contrive to be tolerably comfortable beneath it. Others would groan and sweat and suffer; but the dusky blight would remain, and their lives would be lives of misery. Here and there an individual, irritated beyond endurance, would throw it off in anger, plunging probably into what would be deemed deeper abysses of depravity. Hawthorne's way was the best, for he contrived, by an exquisite process, best known to himself, to transmute this heavy moral burden into the very substance of the imagination, to make it evaporate in the light and charming fumes of artistic production. But Hawthorne, of course, was exceptionally fortunate; he had his genius to help him. Nothing is more curious and interesting than this almost exclusively *imported* character of the sense of sin in Hawthorne's mind; it seems to exist there merely for an artistic or literary purpose. He had ample cognizance of the Puritan conscience; it was his natural heritage; it was reproduced in him; looking into his soul, he found it there. But his relation to it was only, as one may say, intellectual; it was not moral and

theological. He played with it and used it as a pig-
ment; he treated it, as the metaphysicians say, objectively. He was not discomposed, disturbed, haunted
by it, in the manner of its usual and regular victims,
who had not the little postern door of fancy to slip
through, to the other side of the wall. It was, indeed,
to his imaginative vision, the great fact of man's
nature; the light element that had been mingled with
his own composition always clung to this rugged
prominence of moral responsibility, like the mist that
hovers about the mountain. It was a necessary condition for a man of Hawthorne's stock that if his imagination should take licence to amuse itself, it should at
least select this grim precinct of the Puritan morality
for its play-ground. He speaks of the dark disapproval
with which his old ancestors, in the case of their coming
to life, would see him trifling himself away as a story-
teller. But how far more darkly would they have
frowned could they have understood that he had converted the very principle of their own being into one of
his toys !

It will be seen that I am far from being struck with
the justice of that view of the author of the *Twice-Told
Tales*, which is so happily expressed by the French
critic to whom I alluded at an earlier stage of this
essay. To speak of Hawthorne, as M. Emile Montégut
does, as a *romancier pessimiste*, seems to me very much
beside the mark. He is no more a pessimist than an
optimist, though he is certainly not much of either. He
does not pretend to conclude, or to have a philosophy
of human nature; indeed, I should even say that at bot-
tom he does not take human nature as hard as he may
seem to do. " His bitterness," says M. Montégut, "is

without abatement, and his bad opinion of man is without compensation. . . . . His little tales have the air of
confessions which the soul makes to itself ; they are
so many little slaps which the author applies to our
face." This, it seems to me, is to exaggerate almost
immeasurably the reach of Hawthorne's relish of
gloomy subjects. What pleased him in such subjects
was their picturesqueness, their rich duskiness of colour,
their chiaroscuro ; but they were not the expression
of a hopeless, or even of a predominantly melancholy,
feeling about the human soul. Such at least is my own
impression. He is to a considerable degree ironical—
this is part of his charm—part even, one may say, of
his brightness ; but he is neither bitter nor cynical—he
is rarely even what I should call tragical. There have
certainly been story-tellers of a gayer and lighter spirit ;
there have been observers more humorous, more hilarious
—though on the whole Hawthorne's observation has a
smile in it oftener than may at first appear ; but there
has rarely been an observer more serene, less agitated
by what he sees and less disposed to call things deeply
into question. As I have already intimated, his Note-
Books are full of this simple and almost childlike serenity.
That dusky pre-occupation with the misery of human
life and the wickedness of the human heart which such
a critic as M. Emile Montégut talks about, is totally
absent from them ; and if we may suppose a person to have
read these Diaries before looking into the tales, we may
be sure that such a reader would be greatly surprised to
hear the author described as a disappointed, disdainful
genius. " This marked love of cases of conscience,"
says M. Montégut, " this taciturn, scornful cast of
mind, this habit of seeing sin everywhere and hell

always gaping open, this dusky gaze bent always upon
a damned world and a nature draped in mourning,
these lonely conversations of the imagination with the
conscience, this pitiless analysis resulting from a perpetual examination of one's self, and from the tortures
of a heart closed before men and open to God—all
these elements of the Puritan character have passed
into Mr. Hawthorne, or to speak more justly, have
filtered into him, through a long succession, of generations." This is a very pretty and very vivid account of
Hawthorne, superficially considered ; and it is just such
a view of the case as would commend itself most easily
and most naturally to a hasty critic. It is all true indeed, with a difference ; Hawthorne was all that M.
Montégut says, *minus* the conviction. The old Puritan
moral sense, the consciousness of sin and hell, of the
fearful nature of our responsibilities and the savage
character of our Taskmaster—these things had been
lodged in the mind of a man of Fancy, whose fancy
had straightway begun to take liberties and play tricks
with them—to judge them (Heaven forgive him !) from
the poetic and æsthetic point of view, the point of view
of entertainment and irony. This absence of conviction makes the difference ; but the difference is great.

Hawthorne was a man of fancy, and I suppose that
in speaking of him it is inevitable that we should feel
ourselves confronted with the familiar problem of the
difference between the fancy and the imagination. Of
the larger and more potent faculty he certainly possessed a liberal share ; no one can read *The House of
the Seven Gables* without feeling it to be a deeply imaginative work. But I am often struck, especially in the
shorter tales, of which I am now chiefly speaking, with

a kind of small ingenuity, a taste for conceits and analogies, which bears more particularly what is called the fanciful stamp. The finer of the shorter tales are redolent of a rich imagination.

" Had Goodman Brown fallen asleep in the forest and only dreamed a wild dream of witch-meeting ? Be it so, if you will ; but, alas, it was a dream of evil omen for young Goodman Brown ! a stern, a sad, a darkly meditative, a distrustful, if not a desperate, man, did he become from the night of that fearful dream. On the Sabbath-day, when the congregation were singing a holy psalm, he could not listen, because an anthem of sin rushed loudly upon his ear and drowned all the blessed strain. When the minister spoke from the pulpit, with power and fervid eloquence, and with his hand on the open Bible of the sacred truth of our religion, and of saint-like lives and triumphant deaths, and of future bliss or misery unutterable, then did Goodman Brown grow pale, dreading lest the roof should thunder down upon the gray blasphemer and his hearers. Often, awaking suddenly at midnight, he shrank from the bosom of Faith; and at morning or eventide, when the family knelt down at prayer, he scowled and muttered to himself, and gazed sternly at his wife, and turned away. And when he had lived long, and was borne to his grave a hoary corpse, followed by Faith, an aged woman, and children, and grandchildren, a goodly procession, besides neighbours not a few, they carved no hopeful verse upon his tombstone, for his dying hour was gloom."

There is imagination in that, and in many another passage that I might quote ; but as a general thing I should characterise the more metaphysical of our author's short stories as graceful and felicitous conceits. They seem to me to be qualified in this manner by the very fact that they belong to the province of allegory. Hawthorne, in his metaphysical moods, is nothing if not allegorical, and allegory, to my sense, is quite one of the

lighter exercises of the imagination. Many excellent
judges, I know, have a great stomach for it; they
delight in symbols and correspondences, in seeing a story
told as if it were another and a very different story. I
frankly confess that I have as a general thing but little
enjoyment of it and that it has never seemed to me to
be, as it were, a first-rate literary form. It has produced
assuredly some first-rate works; and Hawthorne in his
younger years had been a great reader and devotee of
Bunyan and Spenser, the great masters of allegory.
But it is apt to spoil two good things—a story and a
moral, a meaning and a form; and the taste for it is
responsible for a large part of the forcible-feeble writing
that has been inflicted upon the world. The only cases
in which it is endurable is when it is extremely spontaneous, when the analogy presents itself with eager
promptitude. When it shows signs of having been
groped and fumbled for, the needful illusion is of
course absent and the failure complete. Then the
machinery alone is visible, and the end to which it
operates becomes a matter of indifference. There was
but little literary criticism in the United States at the
time Hawthorne's earlier works were published; but
among the reviewers Edgar Poe perhaps held the
scales the highest. He at any rate rattled them
loudest, and pretended, more than any one else, to
conduct the weighing-process on scientific principles.
Very remarkable was this process of Edgar Poe's, and
very extraordinary were his principles; but he had the
advantage of being a man of genius, and his intelligence
was frequently great. His collection of critical sketches
of the American writers flourishing in what M. Taine
would call his *milieu* and *moment*, is very curious and

interesting reading, and it has one quality which ought
to keep it from ever being completely forgotten. It is
probably the most complete and exquisite specimen of
provincialism ever prepared for the edification of men.
Poe's judgments are pretentious, spiteful, vulgar; but
they contain a great deal of sense and discrimination
as well, and here and there, sometimes at frequent
intervals, we find a phrase of happy insight imbedded
in a patch of the most fatuous pedantry. He wrote a
chapter upon Hawthorne, and spoke of him on the whole
very kindly; and his estimate is of sufficient value to
make it noticeable that he should express lively disapproval of the large part allotted to allegory in his tales
—in defence of which, he says, " however, or for whatever object employed, there is scarcely one respectable
word to be said. . . . . The deepest emotion," he goes
on, " aroused within us by the happiest allegory *as*
allegory, is a very, *very* imperfectly satisfied sense of
the writer's ingenuity in overcoming a difficulty we
should have preferred his not having attempted to
overcome. . . . . One thing is clear, that if allegory
ever establishes a fact, it is by dint of overturning a
fiction ; " and Poe has furthermore the courage to remark that the *Pilgrim's Progress* is a " ludicrously over-
rated book." Certainly, as a general thing, we are
struck with the ingenuity and felicity of Hawthorne's
analogies and correspondences ; the idea appears to have
made itself at home in them easily. Nothing could be
better in this respect than *The Snow-Image* (a little
masterpiece), or *The Great Carbuncle*, or *Doctor Heideg-
ger's Experiment*, or *Rappacini's Daughter*. But in such
things as *The Birth-Mark* and *The Bosom-Serpent*, we are
struck with something stiff and mechanical, slightly

incongruous, as if the kernel had not assimilated its envelope. But these are matters of light impression, and there would be a want of tact in pretending to discriminate too closely among things which all, in one way or another, have a charm. The charm—the great charm—is that they are glimpses of a great field, of the whole deep mystery of man's soul and conscience. They are moral, and their interest is moral ; they deal with something more than the mere accidents and conventionalities, the surface occurrences of life. The fine thing in Hawthorne is that he cared for the deeper psychology, and that, in his way, he tried to become familiar with it. This natural, yet fanciful familiarity with it, this air, on the author's part, of being a confirmed *habitué* of a region of mysteries and subtleties, constitutes the originality of his tales. And then they have the further merit of seeming, for what they are, to spring up so freely and lightly. The author has all the ease, indeed, of a regular dweller in the moral, psychological realm ; he goes to and fro in it, as a man who knows his way. His tread is a light and modest one, but he keeps the key in his pocket.

His little historical stories all seem to me admirable ; they are so good that you may re-read them many times. They are not numerous, and they are very short ; but they are full of a vivid and delightful sense of the New England past ; they have, moreover, the distinction, little tales of a dozen and fifteen pages as they are, of being the only successful attempts at historical fiction that have been made in the United States. Hawthorne was at home in the early New England history ; he had thumbed its records and he had breathed its air, in whatever odd receptacles this somewhat pungent compound

F

still lurked. He was fond of it, and he was proud of
it, as any New Englander must be, measuring the part
of that handful of half-starved fanatics who formed his
earliest precursors, in laying the foundations of a mighty
empire. Hungry for the picturesque as he always was, and
not finding any very copious provision of it around him,
he turned back into the two preceding centuries, with
the earnest determination that the primitive annals of
Massachusetts should at least *appear* picturesque. His
fancy, which was always alive, played a little with the
somewhat meagre and angular facts of the colonial period
and forthwith converted a great many of them into impressive legends and pictures. There is a little infusion
of colour, a little vagueness about certain details, but it
is very gracefully and discreetly done, and realities are
kept in view sufficiently to make us feel that if we are
reading romance, it is romance that rather supplements
than contradicts history. The early annals of New
England were not fertile in legend, but Hawthorne laid
his hands upon everything that would serve his purpose,
and in two or three cases his version of the story has a
great deal of beauty. *The Grey Champion* is a sketch of
less than eight pages, but the little figures stand up in
the tale as stoutly, at the least, as if they were propped
up on half-a-dozen chapters by a dryer annalist, and the
whole thing has the merit of those cabinet pictures in
which the artist has been able to make his persons look
the size of life. Hawthorne, to say it again, was not in
the least a realist—he was not to my mind enough of
one ; but there is no genuine lover of the good city of
Boston but will feel grateful to him for his courage in
attempting to recount the " traditions " of Washington
Street, the main thoroughfare of the Puritan capital.

The four *Legends of the Province House* are certain
shadowy stories which he professes to have gathered in
an ancient tavern lurking behind the modern shop-fronts
of this part of the city. The Province House disap-
peared some years ago, but while it stood it was pointed
to as the residence of the Royal Governors of Massachusetts before the Revolution. I have no recollection
of it, but it cannot have been, even from Hawthorne's
account of it, which is as pictorial as he ventures to
make it, a very imposing piece of antiquity. The
writer's charming touch, however, throws a rich brown
tone over its rather shallow venerableness ; and we are
beguiled into believing, for instance, at the close of
Howe's Masquerade (a story of a strange occurrence at an
entertainment given by Sir William Howe, the last of
the Royal Governors, during the siege of Boston by
Washington), that "superstition, among other legends
of this mansion, repeats the wondrous tale that on the
anniversary night of Britain's discomfiture the ghosts of
the ancient governors of Massachusetts still glide through
the Province House. And last of all comes a figure
shrouded in a military cloak, tossing his clenched hands
into the air and stamping his iron-shod boots upon the
freestone steps, with a semblance of feverish despair,
but without the sound of a foot-tramp." Hawthorne
had, as regards the two earlier centuries of New England
life, that faculty which is called now-a-days the historic
consciousness. He never sought to exhibit it on a large
scale ; he exhibited it indeed on a scale so minute that
we must not linger too much upon it. His vision of the
past was filled with definite images—images none the
less definite that they were concerned with events as
shadowy as this dramatic passing away of the last of

F 2

King George's representatives in his long loyal but
finally alienated colony.

I have said that Hawthorne had become engaged in
about his thirty-fifth year; but he was not married
until 1842. Before this event took place he passed
through two episodes which (putting his falling in love
aside) were much the most important things that had
yet happened to him. They interrupted the painful
monotony of his life, and brought the affairs of men
within his personal experience. One of these was moreover in itself a curious and interesting chapter of observation, and it fructified, in Hawthorne's memory,
in one of his best productions. How urgently he needed
at this time to be drawn within the circle of social accidents, a little anecdote related by Mr. Lathrop in connection with his first acquaintance with the young lady he
was to marry, may serve as an example. This young
lady became known to him through her sister, who had
first approached him as an admirer of the *Twice-Told
Tales* (as to the authorship of which she had been so
much in the dark as to have attributed it first, con-
jecturally, to one of the two Miss Hathornes); and the
two Miss Peabodys, desiring to see more of the charming
writer, caused him to be invited to a species of *conver-
sazione* at the house of one of their friends, at which
they themselves took care to be punctual. Several other
ladies, however, were as punctual as they, and Hawthorne
presently arriving, and seeing a bevy of admirers where
he had expected but three or four, fell into a state of
agitation, which is vividly described by his biographer.
He "stood perfectly motionless, but with the look of a
sylvan creature on the point of fleeing away . . . . He
was stricken with dismay; his face lost colour and took

on a warm paleness . . . . his agitation was very great;
he stood by a table and, taking up some small object
that lay upon it, he found his hand trembling so that he
was obliged to lay it down." It was desirable, certainly,
that something should occur to break the spell of a diffi-
dence that might justly be called morbid. There is
another little sentence dropped by Mr. Lathrop in relation to this period of Hawthorne's life, which appears to
me worth quoting, though I am by no means sure that
it will seem so to the reader. It has a very simple and
innocent air, but to a person not without an impression
of the early days of " culture " in New England, it will
be pregnant with historic meaning. The elder Miss
Peabody, who afterwards was Hawthorne's sister-in-
law and who acquired later in life a very honourable
American fame as a woman of benevolence, of learning,
and of literary accomplishment, had invited the Miss
Hathornes to come to her house for the evening, and
to bring with them their brother, whom she wished to
thank for his beautiful tales. "Entirely to her surprise," says Mr. Lathrop, completing thereby his picture
of the attitude of this remarkable family toward society
—" entirely to her surprise they came. She herself
opened the door, and there, before her, between his
sisters, stood a splendidly handsome youth, tall and
strong, with no appearance whatever of timidity, but
instead, an almost fierce determination making his face
stern. This was his resource for carrying off the extreme inward tremor which he really felt. His hostess
brought out Flaxman's designs for Dante, just received
from Professor Felton, of Harvard, and the party
made an evening's entertainment out of them." This
last sentence is the one I allude to ; and were it not for

fear of appearing too fanciful I should say that these
few words were, to the initiated mind, an unconscious
expression of the lonely frigidity which characterised
most attempts at social recreation in the New England
world some forty years ago. There was at that time a
great desire for culture, a great interest in knowledge,
in art, in æsthetics, together with a very scanty supply
of the materials for such pursuits. Small things were
made to do large service; and there is something
even touching in the solemnity of consideration that
was bestowed by the emancipated New England conscience upon little wandering books and prints, little
echoes and rumours of observation and experience.
There flourished at that time in Boston a very remarkable and interesting woman, of whom we shall have
more to say, Miss Margaret Fuller by name. This lady
was the apostle of culture, of intellectual curiosity, and
in the peculiarly interesting account of her life, published
in 1852 by Emerson and two other of her friends, there
are pages of her letters and diaries which narrate her
visits to the Boston Athenæum and the emotions aroused
in her mind by turning over portfolios of engravings.
These emotions were ardent and passionate — could
hardly have been more so had she been prostrate with
contemplation in the Sistine Chapel or in one of the
chambers of the Pitti Palace. The only analogy I can
recall to this earnestness of interest in great works of
art at a distance from them, is furnished by the great
Goethe's elaborate study of plaster-casts and pencil-
drawings at Weimar. I mention Margaret Fuller
here because a glimpse of her state of mind—her
vivacity of desire and poverty of knowledge—helps to
define the situation. The situation lives for a moment

in those few words of Mr. Lathrop's. The initiated
mind, as I have ventured to call it, has a vision of a
little unadorned parlour, with the snow-drifts of a Massachusetts winter piled up about its windows, and a
group of sensitive and serious people, modest votaries
of opportunity, fixing their eyes upon a bookful of
Flaxman's attenuated outlines.

At the beginning of the year 1839 he received, through
political interest, an appointment as weigher and gauger
in the Boston Custom-house. Mr. Van Buren then occupied the Presidency, and it appears that the Democratic
party, whose successful candidate he had been, rather
took credit for the patronage it had bestowed upon
literary men. Hawthorne was a Democrat, and apparently a zealous one; even in later years, after the
Whigs had vivified their principles by the adoption of
the Republican platform, and by taking up an honest
attitude on the question of slavery, his political faith
never wavered. His Democratic sympathies were eminently natural, and there would have been an incongruity
in his belonging to the other party. He was not only
by conviction, but personally and by association, a
Democrat. When in later years he found himself in
contact with European civilisation, he appears to have
become conscious of a good deal of latent radicalism in
his disposition ; he was oppressed with the burden of
antiquity in Europe, and he found himself sighing for
lightness and freshness and facility of change. But
these things are relative to the point of view, and in
his own country Hawthorne cast his lot with the party
of conservatism, the party opposed to change and
freshness. The people who found something musty and
mouldy in his literary productions would have regarded

this quite as a matter of course; but we are not obliged
to use invidious epithets in describing his political
preferences. The sentiment that attached him to the
Democracy was a subtle and honourable one, and the
author of an attempt to sketch a portrait of him,
should be the last to complain of this adjustment of his
sympathies. It falls much more smoothly into his
reader's conception of him than any other would do;
and if he had had the perversity to be a Republican, I
am afraid our ingenuity would have been considerably
taxed in devising a proper explanation of the circumstance. At any rate, the Democrats gave him a small
post in the Boston Custom-house, to which an annual
salary of $1,200 was attached, and Hawthorne appears
at first to have joyously welcomed the gift. The duties
of the office were not very congruous to the genius of a
man of fancy; but it had the advantage that it broke
the spell of his cursed solitude, as he called it, drew
him away from Salem, and threw him, comparatively
speaking, into the world. The first volume of the
American Note-Books contains some extracts from
letters written during his tenure of this modest office,
which indicate sufficiently that his occupations cannot
have been intrinsically gratifying.

"I have been measuring coal all day," he writes, during
the winter of 1840, "on board of a black little British
schooner, in a dismal dock at the north end of the city.
Most of the time I paced the deck to keep myself warm;
for the wind (north-east, I believe) blew up through the dock
as if it had been the pipe of a pair of bellows. The vessel
lying deep between two wharves, there was no more delightful prospect, on the right hand and on the left, than the posts
and timbers, half immersed in the water and covered with
ice, which the rising and falling of successive tides had

left upon them, so that they looked like immense icicles.
Across the water, however, not more than half a mile off,
appeared the Bunker's Hill Monument, and what interested
me considerably more, a church-steeple, with the dial of a
clock upon it, whereby I was enabled to measure the march
of the weary hours. Sometimes I descended into the dirty
little cabin of the schooner, and warmed myself by a red-hot
stove, among biscuit-barrels, pots and kettles, sea-chests, and
innumerable lumber of all sorts—my olfactories meanwhile
being greatly refreshed with the odour of a pipe, which the
captain, or some one of his crew, was smoking. But at last
came the sunset, with delicate clouds, and a purple light upon
the islands ; and I blessed it, because it was the signal of my
release."

A worse man than Hawthorne would have measured
coal quite as well, and of all the dismal tasks to which
an unremunerated imagination has ever had to accommodate itself, I remember none more sordid than the
business depicted in the foregoing lines. "I pray," he
writes some weeks later, " that in one year more I may
find some way of escaping from this unblest Custom-
house ; for it is a very grievous thraldom. I do detest
all offices ; all, at least, that are held on a political
tenure, and I want nothing to do with politicians.
Their hearts wither away and die out of their bodies.
Their consciences are turned to india-rubber, or to some
substance as black as that and which will stretch as
much. One thing, if no more, I have gained by my
Custom-house experience—to know a politician. It is
a knowledge which no previous thought or power of
sympathy could have taught me ; because the animal,
or the machine rather, is not in nature." A few days
later he goes on in the same strain :—

" I do not think it is the doom laid upon me of murdering
so many of the brightest hours of the day at the Custom-

house that makes such havoc with my wits, for here I am again trying to write worthily . . . . yet with a sense as if all the noblest part of man had been left out of my composition, or had decayed out of it since my nature was given to my own keeping. . . . . Never comes any bird of Paradise into that dismal region. A salt or even a coal-ship is ten million times preferable ; for there the sky is above me, and the fresh breeze around me, and my thoughts having hardly anything to do with my occupation, are as free as air. Nevertheless . . . . it is only once in a while that the image and desire of a better and happier life makes me feel the iron of my chain ; for after all a human spirit may find no insufficiency of food for it, even in the Custom-house. And with such materials as these I do think and feel and learn things that are worth knowing, and which I should not know unless I had learned them there ; so that the present position of my life shall not be quite left out of the sum of my real existence. . . . . It is good for me, on many accounts, that my life has had this passage in it. I know much more than I did a year ago. I have a stronger sense of power to act as a man among men. I have gained worldly wisdom, and wisdom also that is not altogether of this world. And when I quit this earthy career where I am now buried, nothing will cling to me that ought to be left behind. Men will not perceive, I trust, by my look or the tenor of my thoughts and feelings, that I have been a Custom-house officer."

He says, writing shortly afterwards, that "when I shall be free again, I will enjoy all things with the fresh simplicity of a child of five years old. I shall grow young again, made all over anew. I will go forth and stand in a summer shower, and all the worldly dust that has collected on me shall be washed away at once, and my heart will be like a bank of fresh flowers for the weary to rest upon."

This forecast of his destiny was sufficiently exact. A year later, in April 1841, he went to take up his abode

in the socialistic community of Brook Farm.   Here he
found himself among fields and flowers and other natural
products—as well as among many products that could
not very justly be called natural.   He was exposed to
summer showers in plenty ; and his personal associations were as different as possible from those he had
encountered in fiscal circles.   He made acquaintance
with Transcendentalism and the Transcendentalists.

CHAPTER IV.

BROOK FARM AND CONCORD.

THE history of the little industrial and intellectual association which formed itself at this time in one of the suburbs of Boston has not, to my knowledge, been written; though it is assuredly a curious and interesting chapter in the domestic annals of New England. It would of course be easy to overrate the importance of this ingenious attempt of a few speculative persons to improve the outlook of mankind. The experiment came and went very rapidly and quietly, leaving very few traces behind it. It became simply a charming personal reminiscence for the small number of amiable enthusiasts who had had a hand in it. There were degrees of enthusiasm, and I suppose there were degrees of amiability; but a certain generous brightness of hope and freshness of conviction pervaded the whole undertaking and rendered it, morally speaking, important to an extent of which any heed that the world in general ever gave to it is an insufficient measure. Of course it would be a great mistake to represent the episode of Brook Farm as directly related to the manners and morals of the New England world in general—and in especial to those of the prosperous, opulent, comfortable

part of it.   The thing was the experiment of a coterie
—it was unusual, unfashionable, unsuccessful.   It was,
as would then have been said, an amusement of the
Transcendentalists—a harmless effusion of Radicalism.
The Transcendentalists were not, after all, very numerous ; and the Radicals were by no means of the vivid
tinge of those of our own day.   I have said that the
Brook Farm community left no traces behind it that
the world in general can appreciate ; I should rather
say that the only trace is a short novel, of which the
principal merits reside in its qualities of difference from
the affair itself.   *The Blithedale Romance* is the main
result of Brook Farm ; but *The Blithedale Romance* was
very properly never recognised by the Brook Farmers
as an accurate portrait of their little colony.

Nevertheless, in a society as to which the more
frequent complaint is that it is monotonous, that it
lacks variety of incident and of type, the episode, our
own business with which is simply that it was the cause
of Hawthorne's writing an admirable tale, might be
welcomed as a picturesque variation.   At the same time,
if we do not exaggerate its proportions, it may seem
to contain a fund of illustration as to that phase of
human life with which our author's own history mingled
itself.   The most graceful account of the origin of
Brook Farm is probably to be found in these words
of one of the biographers of Margaret Fuller : " In
Boston and its vicinity, several friends, for whose character Margaret felt the highest honour, were earnestly
considering the possibility of making such industrial,
social, and educational arrangements as would simplify
economies, combine leisure for study with healthful
and honest toil, avert unjust collisions of caste, equalise

refinements, awaken generous affections, diffuse courtesy,
and sweeten and sanctify life as a whole." The reader
will perceive that this was a liberal scheme, and that
if the experiment failed, the greater was the pity. The
writer goes on to say that a gentleman, who afterwards distinguished himself in literature (he had begun
by being a clergyman), "convinced by his experience
in a faithful ministry that the need was urgent for
a thorough application of the professed principles of
Fraternity to actual relations, was about staking his
all of fortune, reputation, and influence, in an attempt
to organize a joint-stock company at Brook Farm." As
Margaret Fuller passes for having suggested to Hawthorne the figure of Zenobia in *The Blithedale Romance*,
and as she is probably, with one exception, the person
connected with the affair who, after Hawthorne, offered
most of what is called a personality to the world, I may
venture to quote a few more passages from her Memoirs
—a curious, in some points of view almost a grotesque,
and yet, on the whole, as I have said, an extremely
interesting book. It was a strange history and a strange
destiny, that of this brilliant, restless, and unhappy
woman—this ardent New Englander, this impassioned
Yankee, who occupied so large a place in the thoughts,
the lives, the affections, of an intelligent and appreciative society, and yet left behind her nothing but the
memory of a memory. Her function, her reputation,
were singular, and not altogether reassuring : she was
a talker, she was *the* talker, she was the genius of talk.
She had a magnificent, though by no means an unmiti-
gated, egotism ; and in some of her utterances it is
difficult to say whether pride or humility prevails—as
for instance when she writes that she feels " that there

is plenty of room in the Universe for my faults, and as
if I could not spend time in thinking of them when so
many things interest me more." She has left the same
sort of reputation as a great actress. Some of her
writing has extreme beauty, almost all of it has a real
interest, but her value, her activity, her sway (I am
not sure that one can say her charm), were personal and
practical. She went to Europe, expanded to new desires
and interests, and, very poor herself, married an im-
poverished Italian nobleman. Then, with her husband
and child, she embarked to return to her own country,
and was lost at sea in a terrible storm, within sight of
its coasts. Her tragical death combined with many
of the elements of her life to convert her memory into
a sort of legend, so that the people who had known her
well, grew at last to be envied by later comers. Hawthorne does not appear to have been intimate with her;
on the contrary, I find such an entry as this in the
American Note-Books in 1841 : " I was invited to dine
at Mr. Bancroft's yesterday, with Miss Margaret Fuller ;
but Providence had given me some business to do ; for
which I was very thankful ! " It is true that, later,
the lady is the subject of one or two allusions of a
gentler cast. One of them indeed is so pretty as to be
worth quoting :—

" After leaving the book at Mr. Emerson's, I returned
through the woods, and, entering Sleepy Hollow, I perceived
a lady reclining near the path which bends along its verge. It
was Margaret herself. She had been there the whole afternoon, meditating or reading, for she had a book in her hand
with some strange title which I did not understand and have
forgotten. She said that nobody had broken her solitude,
and was just giving utterance to a theory that no inhabitant
of Concord ever visited Sleepy Hollow, when we saw a

group of people entering the sacred precincts. Most of them
followed a path which led them away from us ; but an old
man passed near us, and smiled to see Margaret reclining on
the ground and me standing by her side. He made some
remark upon the beauty of the afternoon, and withdrew
himself into the shadow of the wood. Then we talked about
autumn, and about the pleasures of being lost in the woods,
and about the crows, whose voices Margaret had heard ; and
about the experiences of early childhood, whose influence
remains upon the character after the recollection of them has
passed away ; and about the sight of mountains from a
distance, and the view from their summits ; and about other
matters of high and low philosophy."

It is safe to assume that Hawthorne could not on
the whole have had a high relish for the very positive
personality of this accomplished and argumentative
woman, in whose intellect high noon seemed ever to
reign, as twilight did in his own. He must have been
struck with the glare of her understanding, and,
mentally speaking, have scowled and blinked a good
deal in conversation with her. But it is tolerably mani-
fest, nevertheless, that she was, in his imagination, the
starting-point of the figure of Zenobia ; and Zenobia is,
to my sense, his only very definite attempt at the
representation of a character. The portrait is full of
alteration and embellishment ; but it has a greater
reality, a greater abundance of detail, than any of his
other figures, and the reality was a memory of the lady
whom he had encountered in the Roxbury pastoral or
among the wood-walks of Concord, with strange books
in her hand and eloquent discourse on her lips. *The
Blithedale Romance* was written just after her unhappy
death, when the reverberation of her talk would lose
much of its harshness. In fact, however, very much

the same qualities that made Hawthorne a Democrat
in politics—his contemplative turn and absence of a
keen perception of abuses, his taste for old ideals, and
loitering paces, and muffled tones—would operate to
keep him out of active sympathy with a woman of the
so-called progressive type. We may be sure that in
women his taste was conservative.

It seems odd, as his biographer says, "that the least
gregarious of men should have been drawn into a
socialistic community;" but although it is apparent
that Hawthorne went to Brook Farm without any
great Transcendental fervour, yet he had various good
reasons for casting his lot in this would-be happy
family. He was as yet unable to marry, but he naturally wished to do so as speedily as possible, and there
was a prospect that Brook Farm would prove an economical residence. And then it is only fair to believe that
Hawthorne was interested in the experiment, and that
though he was not a Transcendentalist, an Abolitionist,
or a Fourierite, as his companions were in some degree
or other likely to be, he was willing, as a generous and
unoccupied young man, to lend a hand in any reasonable scheme for helping people to live together on
better terms than the common. The Brook Farm
scheme was, as such things go, a reasonable one ; it was
devised and carried out by shrewd and sober-minded
New Englanders, who were careful to place economy
first and idealism afterwards, and who were not afflicted
with a Gallic passion for completeness of theory. There
were no formulas, doctrines, dogmas ; there was no
interference whatever with private life or individual
habits, and not the faintest adumbration of a re-
arrangement of that difficult business known as the

G

relations of the sexes. The relations of the sexes
were neither more nor less than what they usually are
in American life, excellent ; and in such particulars the
scheme was thoroughly conservative and irreproachable.
Its main characteristic was that each individual concerned in it should do a part of the work necessary for
keeping the whole machine going. He could choose his
work and he could live as he liked ; it was hoped, but it
was by no means demanded, that he would make himself agreeable, like a gentleman invited to a dinner-
party. Allowing, however, for everything that was a
concession to worldly traditions and to the laxity of
man's nature, there must have been in the enterprise a
good deal of a certain freshness and purity of spirit,
of a certain noble credulity and faith in the per-
fectibility of man, which it would have been easier to
find in Boston in the year 1840, than in London five-
and-thirty years later. If that was the era of Transcendentalism, Transcendentalism could only have
sprouted in the soil peculiar to the general locality of
which I speak—the soil of the old New England
morality, gently raked and refreshed by an imported
culture. The Transcendentalists read a great deal of
French and German, made themselves intimate with
George Sand and Goethe, and many other writers ;
but the strong and deep New England conscience
accompanied them on all their intellectual excursions,
and there never was a so-called "movement" that em-
bodied itself, on the whole, in fewer eccentricities of
conduct, or that borrowed a smaller licence in private
deportment. Henry Thoreau, a delightful writer, went
to live in the woods ; but Henry Thoreau was essentially
a sylvan personage and would not have been, however

the fashion of his time might have turned, a man about town. The brothers and sisters at Brook Farm ploughed the fields and milked the cows ; but I think that an observer from another clime and society would have been much more struck with their spirit of conformity than with their *dérèglements*. Their ardour was a moral ardour, and the lightest breath of scandal never rested upon them, or upon any phase of Transcendentalism.

A biographer of Hawthorne might well regret that his hero had not been more mixed up with the reforming and free-thinking class, so that he might find a pretext for writing a chapter upon the state of Boston society forty years ago. A needful warrant for such regret should be, properly, that the biographer's own personal reminiscences should stretch back to that period and to the persons who animated it. This would be a guarantee of fulness of knowledge and, presumably, of kindness of tone. It is difficult to see, indeed, how the generation of which Hawthorne has given us, in *Blithedale*, a few portraits, should not at this time of day be spoken of very tenderly and sympathetically. If irony enter into the allusion, it should be of the lightest and gentlest. Certainly, for a brief and imperfect chronicler of these things, a writer just touching them as he passes, and who has not the advantage of having been a contemporary, there is only one possible tone. The compiler of these pages, though his recollections date only from a later period, has a memory of a certain number of persons who had been intimately connected, as Hawthorne was not, with the agitations of that interesting time. Something of its interest adhered to them still—something of its aroma clung to their garments; there was something

G 2

about them which seemed to say that when they were
young and enthusiastic, they had been initiated into
moral mysteries, they had played at a wonderful game.
Their usual mark (it is true I can think of exceptions)
was that they seemed excellently good.   They appeared
unstained by the world, unfamiliar with worldly desires
and standards, and with those various forms of human
depravity which flourish in some high phases of civilisation ; inclined to simple and democratic ways, destitute
of pretensions and affectations, of jealousies, of cyni-
cism, of snobbishness.   This little epoch of fermen-
tation has three or four drawbacks for the critic—
drawbacks, however, that may be overlooked by a
person for whom it has an interest of association.   It
bore, intellectually, the stamp of provincialism ; it was
a beginning without a fruition, a dawn without a noon ;
and it produced, with a single exception, no great
talents.   It produced a great deal of writing, but
(always putting Hawthorne aside, as a contemporary
but not a sharer) only one writer in whom the world at
large has interested itself.   The situation was summed
up and transfigured in the admirable and exquisite
Emerson.   He expressed all that it contained, and a
good deal more, doubtless, besides ; he was the man
of genius of the moment ; he was the Transcendentalist
par excellence.   Emerson expressed, before all things,
as was extremely natural at the hour and in the place,
the value and importance of the individual, the duty of
making the most of one's self, of living by one's own
personal light and carrying out one's own disposition.
He reflected with beautiful irony upon the exquisite
impudence of those institutions which claim to have
appropriated the truth, and to dole it out in propor-

tionate morsels, in exchange for a subscription.   He
talked about the beauty and dignity of life, and about
every one who is born into the world being born to the
whole, having an interest and a stake in the whole.
He said "all that is clearly due to-day is not to lie,"
and a great many other things which it would be still
easier to present in a ridiculous light.   He insisted upon
sincerity and independence and spontaneity, upon acting
in harmony with one's nature, and not conforming and
compromising for the sake of being more comfortable.
He urged that a man should await his call, his finding
the thing to do which he should really believe in doing,
and not be urged by the world's opinion to do simply
the world's work.   "If no call should come for years,
for centuries, then I know that the want of the Universe
is the attestation of faith by my abstinence.   .   .   .   If
I cannot work, at least I need not lie."   The doctrine
of the supremacy of the individual to himself, of his
originality and, as regards his own character, *unique*
quality, must have had a great charm for people living
in a society in which introspection, thanks to the want
of other entertainment, played almost the part of a
social resource.

In the United States, in those days, there were no
great things to look out at (save forests and rivers);
life was not in the least spectacular; society was not
brilliant; the country was given up to a great material
prosperity, a homely *bourgeois* activity, a diffusion of
primary education and the common luxuries.   There
was therefore, among the cultivated classes, much relish
for the utterances of a writer who would help one to
take a picturesque view of one's internal possibilities,
and to find in the landscape of the soul all sorts of fine

sunrise and moonlight effects. "Meantime, while the
doors of the temple stand open, night and day, before
every man, and the oracles of this truth cease never,
it is guarded by one stern condition; this, namely—it
is an intuition. It cannot be received at second hand.
Truly speaking, it is not instruction but provocation
that I can receive from another soul." To make one's
self so much more interesting would help to make life
interesting, and life was probably, to many of this
aspiring congregation, a dream of freedom and fortitude.
There were faulty parts in the Emersonian philosophy;
but the general tone was magnificent; and I can easily
believe that, coming when it did and where it did, it
should have been drunk in by a great many fine moral
appetites with a sense of intoxication. One envies, even,
I will not say the illusions, of that keenly sentient
period, but the convictions and interests—the moral
passion. One certainly envies the privilege of having
heard the finest of Emerson's orations poured forth in
their early newness. They were the most poetical, the
most beautiful productions of the American mind, and
they were thoroughly local and national. They had a
music and a magic, and when one remembers the remarkable charm of the speaker, the beautiful modulation
of his utterance, one regrets in especial that one might
not have been present on a certain occasion which made
a sensation, an era—the delivery of an address to the
Divinity School of Harvard University, on a summer
evening in 1838. In the light, fresh American air, un-
thickened and undarkened by customs and institutions
established, these things, as the phrase is, told.

Hawthorne appears, like his own Miles Coverdale,
to have arrived at Brook Farm in the midst of one of

those April snow-storms which, during the New England spring, occasionally diversify the inaction of the
vernal process.   Miles Coverdale, in *The Blithedale
Romance*, is evidently as much Hawthorne as he is any
one else in particular.   He is indeed not very markedly
any one, unless it be the spectator, the observer; his
chief identity lies in his success in looking at things
objectively and spinning uncommunicated fancies about
them.   This indeed was the part that Hawthorne
played socially in the little community at West Rox-
burg.   His biographer describes him as sitting " silently,
hour after hour, in the broad old-fashioned hall of the
house, where he could listen almost unseen to the chat
and merriment of the young people, himself almost
always holding a book before him, but seldom
turning the leaves."   He put his hand to the plough
and supported himself and the community, as they
were all supposed to do, by his labour; but he contributed little to the hum of voices.   Some of his
companions, either then or afterwards, took, I believe,
rather a gruesome view of his want of articulate enthusiasm, and accused him of coming to the place as a sort
of intellectual vampire, for purely psychological purposes.   He sat in a corner, they declared, and watched
the inmates when they were off their guard, analysing
their characters, and dissecting the amiable ardour, the
magnanimous illusions, which he was too cold-blooded
to share.   In so far as this account of Hawthorne's
attitude was a complaint, it was a singularly childish
one.   If he was at Brook Farm without being of it,
this is a very fortunate circumstance from the point
of view of posterity, who would have preserved but a
slender memory of the affair if our author's fine novel

had not kept the topic open. The complaint is indeed
almost so ungrateful a one as to make us regret that
the author's fellow-communists came off so easily. They
certainly would not have done so if the author of
Blithedale had been more of a satirist. Certainly, if
Hawthorne was an observer, he was a very harmless
one ; and when one thinks of the queer specimens of the
reforming genus with which he must have been surrounded, one almost wishes that, for our entertainment,
he had given his old companions something to complain
of in earnest. There is no satire whatever in the
Romance; the quality is almost conspicuous by its
absence. Of portraits there are only two ; there is no
sketching of odd figures—no reproduction of strange
types of radicalism ; the human background is left
vague. Hawthorne was not a satirist, and if at Brook
Farm he was, according to his habit, a good deal of a
mild sceptic, his scepticism was exercised much more in
the interest of fancy than in that of reality.

There must have been something pleasantly bucolic
and pastoral in the habits of the place during the fine
New England summer; but we have no retrospective
envy of the denizens of Brook Farm in that other season
which, as Hawthorne somewhere says, leaves in those
regions, " so large a blank—so melancholy a deathspot
—in lives so brief that they ought to be all summer-
time." " Of a summer night, when the moon was full,"
says Mr. Lathrop, " they lit no lamps, but sat grouped
in the light and shadow, while sundry of the younger
men sang old ballads, or joined Tom Moore's songs to
operatic airs. On other nights there would be an
original essay or poem read aloud, or else a play of
Shakspeare, with the parts distributed to different

members; and these amusements failing, some interesting discussion was likely to take their place.   Occasionally, in the dramatic season, large delegations from
the farm would drive into Boston, in carriages and
waggons, to the opera or the play.   Sometimes, too, the
young women sang as they washed the dishes in the
Hive; and the youthful yeomen of the society came
in and helped them with their work.   The men wore
blouses of a checked or plaided stuff, belted at the
waist, with a broad collar folding down about the
throat, and rough straw hats; the women, usually,
simple calico gowns and hats."   All this sounds de-
lightfully Arcadian and innocent, and it is certain that
there was something peculiar to the clime and race in
some of the features of such a life; in the free, frank,
and stainless companionship of young men and maidens,
in the mixture of manual labour and intellectual flights
—dish-washing and æsthetics, wood-chopping and philosophy.   Wordsworth's " plain living and high thinking "
were made actual.   Some passages in Margaret Fuller's
journals throw plenty of light on this.   (It must be
premised that she was at Brook Farm as an occasional
visitor ; not as a labourer in the Hive.)

" All Saturday I was off in the woods.   In the evening we
had a general conversation, opened by me, upon Education, in
its largest sense, and on what we can do for ourselves and
others.   I took my usual ground :—The aim is perfection;
patience the road.   Our lives should be considered as a
tendency, an approximation only. . . . . Mr. R. spoke admirably on the nature of loyalty.   The people showed a good
deal of the *sans-culotte* tendency in their manners, throwing
themselves on the floor, yawning, and going out when they had
heard enough.   Yet as the majority differ with me, to begin
with—that being the reason this subject was chosen—they

showed on the whole more interest and deference than I
had expected. As I am accustomed to deference; however,
and need it for the boldness and animation which my part
requires, I did not speak with as much force as usual. . . . .
Sunday.—A glorious day ; the woods full of perfume ; I was
out all the morning. In the afternoon Mrs. R. and I had a
talk. I said my position would be too uncertain here, as I
could not work. —— said 'they would all like to work for
a person of genius.' . . . . 'Yes,' I told her ; 'but where
would be my repose when they were always to be judging
whether I was worth it or not ? . . . . Each day you must
prove yourself anew.'. . . . We talked of the principles of
the community. I said I had not a right to come, because all
the confidence I had in it was as an *experiment* worth trying,
and that it was part of the great wave of inspired thought.
. . . . We had valuable discussion on these points. All
Monday morning in the woods again. Afternoon, out with
the drawing party ; I felt the evils of the want of conventional refinement, in the impudence with which one of the
girls treated me. She has since thought of it with regret, I
notice ; and by every day's observation of me will see that
she ought not to have done it. In the evening a husking in
the barn . . . . a most picturesque scene . . . . . I stayed and
helped about half an hour, and then took a long walk beneath
the stars. Wednesday . . . . In the evening a conversation
on Impulse . . . . I defended nature, as I always do ;—the
spirit ascending through, not superseding, nature. But in the
scale of Sense, Intellect, Spirit, I advocated the claims of
Intellect, because those present were rather disposed to post-
pone them. On the nature of Beauty we had good talk.
—— seemed in a much more reverent humour than the other
night, and enjoyed the large plans of the universe which
were unrolled . . . . Saturday.—Well, good-bye, Brook Farm.
I know more about this place than I did when I came ; but the
only way to be qualified for a judge of such an experiment
would be to become an active, though unimpassioned, asso-
ciate in trying it. . . . . The girl who was so rude to me
stood waiting, with a timid air, to bid me good-bye."

The young girl in question cannot have been Hawthorne's charming Priscilla ; nor yet another young lady, of a most humble spirit, who communicated to Margaret's biographers her recollections of this remarkable woman's visits to Brook Farm ; concluding with the assurance that "after a while she seemed to lose sight of my more prominent and disagreeable peculiarities, and treated me with affectionate regard."

Hawthorne's farewell to the place appears to have been accompanied with some reflections of a cast similar to those indicated by Miss Fuller ; in so far at least as we may attribute to Hawthorne himself some of the observations that he fathers upon Miles Coverdale. His biographer justly quotes two or three sentences from *The Blithedale Romance*, as striking the note of the author's feeling about the place. "No sagacious man," says Coverdale, "will long retain his sagacity if he live exclusively among reformers and progressive people, without periodically returning to the settled system of things, to correct himself by a new observation from that old standpoint."   And he remarks elsewhere that "it struck me as rather odd that one of the first questions raised, after our separation from the greedy, struggling, self-seeking world, should relate to the possibility of getting the advantage over the outside barbarians in their own field of labour.   But to tell the truth, I very soon became sensible that, as regarded society at large, we stood in a position of new hostility rather than new brotherhood."   He was doubtless oppressed by the "sultry heat of society," as he calls it in one of the jottings in the Note-Books. "What would a man do if he were compelled to live always in the sultry heat of society, and could never bathe himself in cool solitude ? " His biographer relates that one of the other Brook Farmers, wandering afield one summer's day, discovered Hawthorne stretched at his length upon a grassy hill-side, with his hat pulled over his face, and every appearance, in his attitude, of the desire to escape detection. On his asking him whether he had any particular reason for this shyness of posture — " Too much of a party up there ! " Hawthorne contented himself with replying, with a nod in the direction of the Hive. He had nevertheless for a time looked forward to remaining indefinitely in the community ; he meant to marry as soon as possible and bring his wife there to live. Some sixty pages of the second volume of the American Note-Books are occupied with extracts from his letters to his future wife and from his journal (which appears however at this time to have been only intermittent), consisting almost exclusively of descriptions of the simple scenery of the neighbour-hood, and of the state of the woods and fields and weather. Hawthorne's fondness for all the common things of nature was deep and constant, and there is always something charming in his verbal touch, as we may call it, when he talks to himself about them. "Oh," he breaks out, of an October afternoon, "the beauty of grassy slopes, and the hollow ways of paths winding between hills, and the intervals between the road and wood-lots, where Summer lingers and sits down, strewing dandelions of gold and blue asters as her parting gifts and memorials ! " He was but a single summer at Brook Farm ; the rest of his residence had the winter-quality.

But if he returned to solitude, it was henceforth to be as the French say, a *solitude à deux*. He was married in

July 1842, and betook himself immediately to the ancient village of Concord, near Boston, where he occupied the so-called Manse which has given the title to one of his collections of tales, and upon which this work, in turn, has conferred a permanent distinction. I use the epithets "ancient" and "near" in the foregoing sentence, according to the American measurement of time and distance. Concord is some twenty miles from Boston, and even to-day, upwards of forty years after the date of Hawthorne's removal thither, it is a very fresh and well-preserved looking town. It had already a local history when, a hundred years ago, the larger current of human affairs flowed for a moment around it. Concord has the honour of being the first spot in which blood was shed in the war of the Revolution; here occurred the first exchange of musket-shots between the King's troops and the American insurgents. Here, as Emerson says in the little hymn which he contributed in 1836 to the dedication of a small monument commemorating this circumstance—

> "Here once the embattled farmers stood,
>   And fired the shot heard round the world."

The battle was a small one, and the farmers were not destined individually to emerge from obscurity ; but the memory of these things has kept the reputation of Concord green, and it has been watered, moreover, so to speak, by the life-long presence there of one of the most honoured of American men of letters—the poet from whom I just quoted two lines. Concord is indeed in itself decidedly verdant, and is an excellent specimen of a New England village of the riper sort. At the time of Hawthorne's first going there it must have been an even better specimen than to-day,—more homogeneous,

more indigenous, more absolutely democratic. Forty
years ago the tide of foreign immigration had scarcely
begun to break upon the rural strongholds of the
New England race; it had at most begun to splash
them with the salt Hibernian spray. It is very possible,
however, that at this period there was not an Irishman
in Concord; the place would have been a village community operating in excellent conditions. Such a
village community was not the least honourable item
in the sum of New England civilisation. Its spreading
elms and plain white houses, its generous summers and
ponderous winters, its immediate background of pro-
miscuous field and forest, would have been part of the
composition. For the rest, there were the selectmen
and the town-meetings, the town-schools and the self-
governing spirit, the rigid morality, the friendly and
familiar manners, the perfect competence of the little
society to manage its affairs itself. In the delightful
introduction to the *Mosses*, Hawthorne has given an
account of his dwelling, of his simple occupations and
recreations, and of some of the characteristics of the
place. The Manse is a large, square wooden house, to
the surface of which—even in the dry New Englannd air,
so unfriendly to mosses and lichens and weather-stains,
and the other elements of a picturesque complexion—
a hundred and fifty years of exposure have imparted
a kind of tone, standing just above the slow-flowing
Concord river, and approached by a short avenue of
over-arching trees. It had been the dwelling-place of
generations of Presbyterian ministers, ancestors of the
celebrated Emerson, who had himself spent his early
manhood and written some of his most beautiful essays
there. "He used," as Hawthorne says, "to watch the

Assyrian dawn, and Paphian sunset and moonrise, from
the summit of our eastern hill." From its clerical occu-
pants the place had inherited a mild mustiness of
theological association—a vague reverberation of old
Calvinistic sermons, which served to deepen its extra-
mundane and somnolent quality. The three years that
Hawthorne passed here were, I should suppose, among
the happiest of his life. The future was indeed not in
any special manner assured ; but the present was
sufficiently genial. In the American Note-Books there
is a charming passage (too long to quote) descriptive of
the entertainment the new couple found in renovating
and re-furnishing the old parsonage, which, at the time
of their going into it, was given up to ghosts and cob-
webs. Of the little drawing-room, which had been
most completely reclaimed, he writes that "the shade
of our departed host will never haunt it ; for its aspect
has been as completely changed as the scenery of a
theatre. Probably the ghost gave one peep into it,
uttered a groan, and vanished for ever." This departed host was a certain Doctor Ripley, a venerable
scholar, who left behind him a reputation of learning
and sanctity which was reproduced in one of the ladies
of his family, long the most distinguished woman in the
little Concord circle. Doctor Ripley's predecessor had
been, I believe, the last of the line of the Emerson
ministers—an old gentleman who, in the earlier years of
his pastorate, stood at the window of his study (the same
in which Hawthorne handled a more irresponsible quill)
watching, with his hands under his long coat-tails, the
progress of Concord fight. It is not by any means related,
however, I should add, that he waited for the conclusion
to make up his mind which was the righteous cause.

Hawthorne had a little society (as much, we may infer, as he desired); and it was excellent in quality. But the pages in the Note-Books which relate to his life at the Manse, and the introduction to the *Mosses*, make more of his relations with vegetable nature, and of his customary contemplation of the incidents of wood-path and way-side, than of the human elements of the scene; though these also are gracefully touched upon. These pages treat largely of the pleasures of a kitchen-garden, of the beauty of summer-squashes, and of the mysteries of apple raising. With the wholesome aroma of apples (as is indeed almost necessarily the case in any realistic record of New England rural life) they are especially pervaded; and with many other homely and domestic emanations; all of which derive a sweetness from the medium of our author's colloquial style. Hawthorne was silent with his lips; but he talked with his pen. The tone of his writing is often that of charming talk— ingenious, fanciful, slow-flowing, with all the lightness of gossip, and none of its vulgarity. In the preface to the tales written at the Manse he talks of many things, and just touches upon some of the members of his circle —especially upon that odd genius, his fellow-villager, Henry Thoreau. I said a little way back that the New England Transcendental movement had suffered in the estimation of the world at large from not having (putting Emerson aside) produced any superior talents. But any reference to it would be ungenerous which should omit to pay a tribute in passing to the author of *Walden*. Whatever question there may be of his talent, there can be none, I think, of his genius. It was a slim and crooked one; but it was eminently personal. He was imperfect, unfinished, inartistic; he was worse

than provincial—he was parochial; it is only at his best
that he is readable. But at his best he has an extreme
natural charm, and he must always be mentioned after
those Americans — Emerson, Hawthorne, Longfellow,
Lowell, Motley—who have written originally. He was
Emerson's independent moral man made flesh—living
for the ages, and not for Saturday and Sunday; for
the Universe, and not for Concord. In fact, however,
Thoreau lived for Concord very effectually, and by his
remarkable genius for the observation of the phenomena
of woods and streams, of plants and trees, and beasts
and fishes, and for flinging a kind of spiritual interest
over these things, he did more than he perhaps intended toward consolidating the fame of his accidental
human sojourn. He was as shy and ungregarious as
Hawthorne; but he and the latter appear to have been
sociably disposed towards each other, and there are
some charming touches in the preface to the *Mosses* in
regard to the hours they spent in boating together on
the large, quiet Concord river. Thoreau was a great
voyager, in a canoe which he had constructed himself,
and which he eventually made over to Hawthorne, and
as expert in the use of the paddle as the Red men who
had once haunted the same silent stream. The most
frequent of Hawthorne's companions on these excursions
appears, however, to have been a local celebrity—as well
as Thoreau a high Transcendentalist—Mr. Ellery Chan-
ning, whom I may mention, since he is mentioned very
explicitly in the preface to the *Mosses*, and also because
no account of the little Concord world would be complete which should omit him. He was the son of the
distinguished Unitarian moralist, and, I believe, the
intimate friend of Thoreau, whom he resembled in

H

having produced literary compositions more esteemed
by the few than by the many. He and Hawthorne
were both fishermen, and the two used to set themselves afloat in the summer afternoons. "Strange and
happy times were those," exclaims the more distinguished of the two writers, "when we cast aside all
irksome forms and strait-laced habitudes, and delivered
ourselves up to the free air, to live like the Indians or
any less conventional race, during one bright semi-
circle of the sun. Rowing our boat against the current,
between wide meadows, we turned aside into the Assa-
beth. A more lovely stream than this, for a mile above
its junction with the Concord, has never flowed on
earth — nowhere indeed except to lave the interior
regions of a poet's imagination. . . . . It comes flowing
softly through the midmost privacy and deepest heart
of a wood which whispers it to be quiet; while the
stream whispers back again from its sedgy borders, as
if river and wood were hushing one another to sleep.
Yes ; the river sleeps along its course and dreams of
the sky and the clustering foliage. . . . ." While
Hawthorne was looking at these beautiful things, or,
for that matter, was writing them, he was well out of
the way of a certain class of visitants whom he alludes
to in one of the closing passages of this long Introduction. "Never was a poor little country village infested
with such a variety of queer, strangely-dressed, oddly-
behaved mortals, most of whom took upon themselves
to be important agents of the world's destiny, yet were
simply bores of a very intense character." "These
hobgoblins of flesh and blood," he says in a preceding
paragraph, "were attracted thither by the wide-spread-
ing influence of a great original thinker who had his

earthly abode at the opposite extremity of our village.
. . . . People that had lighted on a new thought or a
thought they fancied new, came to Emerson, as the
finder of a glittering gem hastens to a lapidary, to
ascertain its quality and value." And Hawthorne
enumerates some of the categories of pilgrims to the
shrine of the mystic counsellor, who as a general thing
was probably far from abounding in their own sense
(when this sense was perverted), but gave them a due
measure of plain practical advice. The whole passage
is interesting, and it suggests that little Concord had
not been ill-treated by the fates—with "a great original
thinker" at one end of the village, an exquisite teller
of tales at the other, and the rows of New England
elms between. It contains moreover an admirable
sentence about Hawthorne's pilgrim-haunted neighbour,
with whom, "being happy," as he says, and feeling
therefore "as if there were no question to be put," he
was not in metaphysical communion. "It was good
nevertheless to meet him in the wood-paths, or sometimes in our avenue, with that pure intellectual gleam
diffused about his presence, like the garment of a
shining one; and he so quiet, so simple, so without
pretension, encountering each man alive as if expecting
to receive more than he could impart!" One may without indiscretion risk the surmise that Hawthorne's perception of the "shining" element in his distinguished friend
was more intense than his friend's appreciation of whatever luminous property might reside within the somewhat dusky envelope of our hero's identity as a collector
of "mosses." Emerson, as a sort of spiritual sun-wor-
shipper, could have attached but a moderate value to
Hawthorne's cat-like faculty of seeing in the dark.

" As to the daily course of our life," the latter writes
in the spring of 1843, " I have written with pretty
commendable diligence, averaging from two to four
hours a day ; and the result is seen in various magazines. I might have written more if it had seemed
worth while, but I was content to earn only so much
gold as might suffice for our immediate wants, having
prospect of official station and emolument which would
do away with the necessity of writing for bread. These
prospects have not yet had their fulfilment ; and we are
well content to wait, for an office would inevitably
remove us from our present happy home—at least from
an outward home ; for there is an inner one that will
accompany us wherever we go. Meantime, the magazine people do not pay their debts ; so that we taste
some of the inconveniences of poverty. It is an annoy-
ance, not a trouble." And he goes on to give some
account of his usual habits. (The passage is from his
Journal, and the account is given to himself, as it were,
with that odd, unfamiliar explicitness which marks the
tone of this record throughout.) " Every day I trudge
through snow and slosh to the village, look into the
post-office, and spend an hour at the reading-room ; and
then return home, generally without having spoken a
word to any human being. . . . . In the way of exercise I saw and split wood, and physically I was never
in a better condition than now." He adds a mention
of an absence he had lately made. " I went alone to
Salem, where I resumed all my bachelor habits for
nearly a fortnight, leading the same life in which ten
years of my youth flitted away like a dream. But how
much changed was I ! At last I had got hold of a
reality which never could be taken from me. It was

good thus to get apart from my happiness for the sake
of contemplating it."

These compositions, which were so unpunctually paid
for, appeared in the *Democratic Review*, a periodical
published at Washington, and having, as our author's
biographer says, "considerable pretensions to a national
character." It is to be regretted that the practice of
keeping its creditors waiting should, on the part of the
magazine in question, have been thought compatible
with these pretensions. The foregoing lines are a description of a very monotonous but a very contented
life, and Mr. Lathrop justly remarks upon the dis-
sonance of tone of the tales Hawthorne produced under
these happy circumstances. It is indeed not a little
of an anomaly. The episode of the Manse was one
of the most agreeable he had known, and yet the
best of the *Mosses* (though not the greater number of
them) are singularly dismal compositions. They are
redolent of M. Montégut's pessimism. "The reality
of sin, the pervasiveness of evil," says Mr. Lathrop,
"had been but slightly insisted upon in the earlier
tales : in this series the idea bursts up like a long-
buried fire, with earth-shaking strength, and the pits
of hell seem yawning beneath us." This is very true
(allowing for Mr. Lathrop's rather too emphatic way
of putting it); but the anomaly is, I think, on the
whole, only superficial. Our writer's imagination, as
has been abundantly conceded, was a gloomy one; the
old Puritan sense of sin, of penalties to be paid, of the
darkness and wickedness of life, had, as I have already
suggested, passed into it. It had not passed into the
parts of Hawthorne's nature corresponding to those
occupied by the same horrible vision of things in his

ancestors; but it had still been determined to claim
this later comer as its own, and since his heart and his
happiness were to escape, it insisted on setting its
mark upon his genius—upon his most beautiful organ,
his admirable fancy. It may be said that when his
fancy was strongest and keenest, when it was most
itself, then the dark Puritan tinge showed in it most
richly; and there cannot be a better proof that he was
not the man of a sombre *parti-pris* whom M. Montégut
describes, than the fact that these duskiest flowers of
his invention sprang straigh · from the soil of his
happiest days. This surely indicates that there was
but little direct connection between the products of his
fancy and the state of his affections. When he was
lightest at heart, he was most creative, and when he
was most creative, the moral picturesqueness of the old
secret of mankind in general and of the Puritans in
particular, most appealed to him—the secret that we
are really not by any means so good as a well-regulated
society requires us to appear. It is not too much to
say, even, that the very condition of production of
some of these unamiable tales would be that they
should be superficial, and, as it were, insincere. The
magnificent little romance of *Young Goodman Brown*,
for instance, evidently means nothing as regards Hawthorne's own state of mind, his conviction of human
depravity and his consequent melancholy; for the
simple reason that if it meant anything, it would
mean too much. Mr. Lathrop speaks of it as a
"terrible and lurid parable;" but this, it seems to
me, is just what it is not. It is not a parable, but
a picture, which is a very different thing. What does
M. Montégut make, one would ask, from the point

of view of Hawthorne's pessimism, of the singularly
objective and unpreoccupied tone of the Introduction
to the *Old Manse*, in which the author speaks from
himself, and in which the cry of metaphysical despair
is not even faintly sounded ?

We have seen that when he went into the village he
often came home without having spoken a word to a
human being.   There is a touching entry made a little
later, bearing upon his mild taciturnity.   " A cloudy
veil stretches across the abyss of my nature.   I have,
however, no love of secrecy and darkness.   I am glad
to think that God sees through my heart, and if any
angel has power to penetrate into it, he is welcome to
know everything that is there.   Yes, and so may any
mortal who is capable of full sympathy, and therefore
worthy to come into my depths.   But he must find his
own way there ; I can neither guide nor enlighten him."
It must be acknowledged, however, that if he was not
able to open the gate of conversation, it was sometimes
because he was disposed to slide the bolt himself.   " I
had a purpose," he writes, shortly before the entry last
quoted, "if circumstances would permit, of passing the
whole term of my wife's absence without speaking a
word to any human being."   He beguiled these in-
communicative periods by studying German, in Tieck
and Bürger, without apparently making much progress ;
also in reading French, in Voltaire and Rabelais. "Just
now," he writes, one October noon, " I heard a sharp
tapping at the window of my study, and, looking up
from my book (a volume of Rabelais), behold, the head
of a little bird, who seemed to demand admittance."
It was a quiet life, of course, in which these diminutive
incidents seemed noteworthy ; and what is noteworthy

here to the observer of Hawthorne's contemplative
simplicity, is the fact that though he finds a good deal
to say about the little bird (he devotes several lines
more to it) he makes no remark upon Rabelais. He
had other visitors than little birds, however, and their
demands were also not Rabelaisian. Thoreau comes
to see him, and they talk "upon the spiritual advan-
tages of change of place, and upon the *Dial*, and upon
Mr. Alcott, and other kindred or concatenated subjects."
Mr. Alcott was an arch-transcendentalist, living in
Concord, and the *Dial* was a periodical to which the
illuminated spirits of Boston and its neighbourhood
used to contribute. Another visitor comes and talks
"of Margaret Fuller, who, he says, has risen per-
ceptibly into a higher state since their last meeting."
There is probably a great deal of Concord five-and-
thirty years ago in that little sentence!

CHAPTER V.

THE prospect of official station and emolument which Hawthorne mentions in one of those paragraphs from his Journals which I have just quoted, as having offered itself and then passed away, was at last, in the event, confirmed by his receiving from the administration of President Polk the gift of a place in the Custom-house of his native town.   The office was a modest one, and " official station " may perhaps appear a magniloquent formula for the functions sketched in the admirable Introduction to *The Scarlet Letter*. Hawthorne's duties were those of Surveyor of the port of Salem, and they had a salary attached, which was the important part ; as his biographer tells us that he had received almost nothing for the contributions to the *Democratic Review*. He bade farewell to his ex-parsonage and went back to Salem in 1846, and the immediate effect of his ameliorated fortune was to make him stop writing. None of his Journals of the period from his going to Salem to 1850 have been published ; from which I infer that he even ceased to journalise. *The Scarlet Letter* was not written till 1849. In the delightful prologue to that work, entitled *The Custom-house* he embodies some of the impressions gathered during these years of comparative leisure (I say of leisure because he does not intimate in this sketch of his occupations that his duties were onerous). He intimates, however, that they were not interesting, and that it was a very good thing for him, mentally and morally, when his term of service expired—or rather when he was removed from office by the operation of that wonderful "rotatory" system which his countrymen had invented for the administration of their affairs. This sketch of the Custom-house is, as simple writing, one of the most perfect of Hawthorne's compositions, and one of the most gracefully and humorously autobiographic. It would be interesting to examine it in detail, but I prefer to use my space for making some remarks upon the work which was the ultimate result of this period of Hawthorne's residence in his native town ; and I shall, for convenience' sake, say directly afterwards what I have to say about the two companions of *The Scarlet Letter*—*The House of the Seven Gables* and *The Blithedale Romance*. I quoted some passages from the prologue to the first of these novels in the early pages of this essay. There is another passage, however, which bears particularly upon this phase of Hawthorne's career, and which is so happily expressed as to make it a pleasure to transcribe it—the passage in which he says that "for myself, during the whole of my Custom-house experience, moonlight and sunshine, and the glow of the fire-light, were just alike in my regard, and neither of them was of one whit more avail than the twinkle of a tallow candle. An entire class of susceptibilities, and a gift connected with them—of no great richness or value, but the best I had—was gone from me." He goes on to say that he believes that

he might have done something if he could have made up
his mind to convert the very substance of the commonplace that surrounded him into matter of literature.

"I might, for instance, have contented myself with
writing out the narratives of a veteran shipmaster, one of the
inspectors, whom I should be most ungrateful not to mention ;
since scarcely a day passed that he did not stir me to laughter
and admiration by his marvellous gift as a story-teller. . . . .
Or I might readily have found a more serious task. It was a
folly, with the materiality of this daily life pressing so
intrusively upon me, to attempt to fling myself back into
another age ; or to insist on creating a semblance of a world
out of airy matter. . . . . The wiser effort would have been,
to diffuse thought and imagination through the opaque substance of to-day, and thus make it a bright transparency
. . . . to seek resolutely the true and indestructible value
that lay hidden in the petty and wearisome incidents and
ordinary characters with which I was now conversant. The
fault was mine. The page of life that was spread out before
me was dull and commonplace, only because I had not
fathomed its deeper import. A better book than I shall ever
write was there. . . . . These perceptions came too late.
. . . . I had ceased to be a writer of tolerably poor tales and
essays, and had become a tolerably good Surveyor of the
Customs. That was all. But, nevertheless, it is anything
but agreeable to be haunted by a suspicion that one's intellect
is dwindling away, or exhaling, without your consciousness,
like ether out of phial ; so that at every glance you find a
smaller and less volatile residuum."

As, however, it was with what was left of his intellect
after three years' evaporation, that Hawthorne wrote
The Scarlet Letter, there is little reason to complain of
the injury he suffered in his Surveyorship.

His publisher, Mr. Fields, in a volume entitled
Yesterdays with Authors, has related the circumstances in
which Hawthorne's masterpiece came into the world.

"In the winter of 1849, after he had been ejected from
the Custom-house, I went down to Salem to see him
and inquire after his health, for we heard he had been
suffering from illness. He was then living in a modest
wooden house. . . . I found him alone in a chamber
over the sitting-room of the dwelling, and as the day
was cold he was hovering near a stove. We fell into
talk about his future prospects, and he was, as I feared
I should find him, in a very desponding mood." His
visitor urged him to bethink himself of publishing
something, and Hawthorne replied by calling his attention to the small popularity his published productions
had yet acquired, and declaring that he had done
nothing and had no spirit for doing anything. The
narrator of the incident urged upon him the necessity
of a more hopeful view of his situation, and proceeded
to take leave. He had not reached the street, however,
when Hawthorne hurried to overtake him, and, placing
a roll of MS. in his hand, bade him take it to Boston,
read it, and pronounce upon it. "It is either very
good or very bad," said the author; "I don't know
which." "On my way back to Boston," says Mr.
Fields, "I read the germ of *The Scarlet Letter ;* before
I slept that night I wrote him a note all aglow with
admiration of the marvellous story he had put into my
hands, and told him that I would come again to Salem
the next day and arrange for its publication. I went on in
such an amazing state of excitement, when we met again
in the little house, that he would not believe I was really
in earnest. He seemed to think I was beside myself,
and laughed sadly at my enthusiasm." Hawthorne,
however, went on with the book and finished it, but it
appeared only a year later. His biographer quotes a

passage from a letter which he wrote in February, 1850, to his friend Horatio Bridge. " I finished my book only yesterday ; one end being in the press at Boston, while the other was in my head here at Salem, so that, as you see, my story is at least fourteen miles long. . . My book, the publisher tells me, will not be out before April. He speaks of it in tremendous terms of appro- bation, so does Mrs. Hawthorne, to whom I read the conclusion last night. It broke her heart, and sent her to bed with a grievous headache—which I look upon as a triumphant success. Judging from the effect upon her and the publisher, I may calculate on what bowlers call a ten-strike. But I don't make any such calculation." And Mr. Lathrop calls attention, in regard to this pas- sage, to an allusion in the English Note-Books (Sep- tember 14, 1855). " Speaking of Thackeray, I cannot but wonder at his coolness in respect to his own pathos, and compare it to my emotions when I read the last scene of *The Scarlet Letter* to my wife, just after writing it—tried to read it rather, for my voice swelled and heaved as if I were tossed up and down on an ocean as it subsides after a storm. But I was in a very nervous state then, having gone through a great diversity of emotion while writing it, for many months."

The work has the tone of the circumstances in which it was produced. If Hawthorne was in a sombre mood, and if his future was painfully vague, *The Scarlet Letter* contains little enough of gaiety or of hopefulness. It is densely dark, with a single spot of vivid colour in it ; and it will probably long remain the most consistently gloomy of English novels of the first order. But I just now called it the author's masterpiece, and I imagine it will continue to be, for other generations than ours, his

most substantial title to fame. The subject had probably lain a long time in his mind, as his subjects were
apt to do ; so that he appears completely to possess it,
to know it and feel it. It is simpler and more complete
than his other novels; it achieves more perfectly what
it attempts, and it has about it that charm, very hard to
express, which we find in an artist's work the first time
he has touched his highest mark—a sort of straightness
and naturalness of execution, an unconsciousness of his
public, and freshness of interest in his theme. It was a
great success, and he immediately found himself famous.
The writer of these lines, who was a child at the time,
remembers dimly the sensation the book produced, and
the little shudder with which people alluded to it, as if
a peculiar horror were mixed with its attractions. He
was too young to read it himself, but its title, upon
which he fixed his eyes as the book lay upon the table,
had a mysterious charm. He had a vague belief indeed
that the "letter" in question was one of the documents
that come by the post, and it was a source of perpetual
wonderment to him that it should be of such an unaccustomed hue. Of course it was difficult to explain to
a child the significance of poor Hester Prynne's blood-
coloured *A*. But the mystery was at last partly
dispelled by his being taken to see a collection of pictures (the annual exhibition of the National Academy),
where he encountered a representation of a pale, handsome woman, in a quaint black dress and a white coif,
holding between her knees an elfish-looking little girl,
fantastically dressed and crowned with flowers. Em-
broidered on the woman's breast was a great crimson *A*,
over which the child's fingers, as she glanced strangely
out of the picture, were maliciously playing. I was

told that this was Hester Prynne and little Pearl, and
that when I grew older I might read their interesting
history. But the picture remained vividly imprinted
on my mind; I had been vaguely frightened and made
uneasy by it; and when, years afterwards, I first
read the novel, I seemed to myself to have read it
before, and to be familiar with its two strange heroines.
I mention this incident simply as an indication of the
degree to which the success of *The Scarlet Letter* had
made the book what is called an actuality. Hawthorne
himself was very modest about it; he wrote to his publisher, when there was a question of his undertaking
another novel, that what had given the history of
Hester Prynne its "vogue" was simply the introductory
chapter. In fact, the publication of *The Scarlet Letter*
was in the United States a literary event of the first
importance. The book was the finest piece of imaginative writing yet put forth in the country. There was
a consciousness of this in the welcome that was given
it—a satisfaction in the idea of America having produced a novel that belonged to literature, and to the
forefront of it. Something might at last be sent to
Europe as exquisite in quality as anything that had
been received, and the best of it was that the thing was
absolutely American; it belonged to the soil, to the air;
it came out of the very heart of New England.

It is beautiful, admirable, extraordinary; it has in
the highest degree that merit which I have spoken of
as the mark of Hawthorne's best things—an indefinable
purity and lightness of conception, a quality which in
a work of art affects one in the same way as the absence
of grossness does in a human being. His fancy, as I
just now said, had evidently brooded over the subject

for a long time; the situation to be represented had
disclosed itself to him in all its phases.   When I say in
all its phases, the sentence demands modification; for
it is to be remembered that if Hawthorne laid his
hand upon the well-worn theme, upon the familiar
combination of the wife, the lover, and the husband,
it was after all but to one period of the history
of these three persons that he attached himself.   The
situation is the situation after the woman's fault has
been committed, and the current of expiation and re-
pentance has set in.   In spite of the relation between
Hester Prynne and Arthur Dimmesdale, no story of
love was surely ever less of a "love story."   To Hawthorne's imagination the fact that these two persons
had loved each other too well was of an interest comparatively vulgar; what appealed to him was the idea
of their moral situation in the long years that were to
follow.   The story indeed is in a secondary degree that
of Hester Prynne; she becomes, really, after the first
scene, an accessory figure; it is not upon her the *dénoûment* depends.   It is upon her guilty lover that the
author projects most frequently the cold, thin rays of
his fitfully-moving lantern, which makes here and there
a little luminous circle, on the edge of which hovers
the livid and sinister figure of the injured and retri-
butive husband.   The story goes on for the most part
between the lover and the husband—the tormented
young Puritan minister, who carries the secret of his
own lapse from pastoral purity locked up beneath an
exterior that commends itself to the reverence of his
flock, while he sees the softer partner of his guilt
standing in the full glare of exposure and humbling
herself to the misery of atonement—between this more

wretched and pitiable culprit, to whom dishonour would
come as a comfort and the pillory as a relief, and the
older, keener, wiser man, who, to obtain satisfaction
for the wrong he has suffered, devises the infernally
ingenious plan of conjoining himself with his wronger,
living with him, living upon him, and while he pretends
to minister to his hidden ailment and to sympathise
with his pain, revels in his unsuspected knowledge
of these things and stimulates them by malignant arts.
The attitude of Roger Chillingworth, and the means
he takes to compensate himself—these are the highly
original elements in the situation that Hawthorne so
ingeniously treats.   None of his works are so impregnated with that after-sense of the old Puritan consciousness of life to which allusion has so often been
made.   If, as M. Montégut says, the qualities of his
ancestors *filtered* down through generations into his
composition, *The Scarlet Letter* was, as it were, the
vessel that gathered up the last of the precious drops.
And I say this not because the story happens to be of
so-called historical cast, to be told of the early days
of Massachusetts and of people in steeple-crowned hats
and sad-coloured garments.   The historical colouring is
rather weak than otherwise ; there is little elaboration
of detail, of the modern realism of research ; and the
author has made no great point of causing his figures to
speak the English of their period.   Nevertheless, the
book is full of the moral presence of the race that
invented Hester's penance—diluted and complicated
with other things, but still perfectly recognisable.
Puritanism, in a word, is there, not only objectively,
as Hawthorne tried to place it there, but subjectively
as well.   Not, I mean, in his judgment of his characters,

I

in any harshness of prejudice, or in the obtrusion of a moral lesson ; but in the very quality of his own vision, in the tone of the picture, in a certain coldness and exclusiveness of treatment.

The faults of the book are, to my sense, a want of reality and an abuse of the fanciful element—of a certain superficial symbolism. The people strike me not as characters, but as representatives, very picturesquely arranged, of a single state of mind ; and the interest of the story lies, not in them, but in the situation, which is insistently kept before us, with little progression, though with a great deal, as I have said, of a certain stable variation ; and to which they, out of their reality, contribute little that helps it to live and move. I was made to feel this want of reality, this over-ingenuity, of *The Scarlet Letter*, by chancing not long since upon a novel which was read fifty years ago much more than to-day, but which is still worth reading—the story of *Adam Blair*, by John Gibson Lockhart. This interesting and powerful little tale has a great deal of analogy with Hawthorne's novel —quite enough, at least, to suggest a comparison between them ; and the comparison is a very interesting one to make, for it speedily leads us to larger considerations than simple resemblances and divergences of plot.

Adam Blair, like Arthur Dimmesdale, is a Calvinistic minister who becomes the lover of a married woman, is overwhelmed with remorse at his misdeed, and makes a public confession of it ; then expiates it by resigning his pastoral office and becoming a humble tiller of the soil, as his father had been. The two stories are of about the same length, and each is the masterpiece

(putting aside of course, as far as Lockhart is concerned, the *Life of Scott*) of the author. They deal
alike with the manners of a rigidly theological society,
and even in certain details they correspond. In each
of them, between the guilty pair, there is a charming
little girl; though I hasten to say that Sarah Blair
(who is not the daughter of the heroine but the legiti-
mate offspring of the hero, a widower) is far from being
as brilliant and graceful an apparition as the admirable
little Pearl of *The Scarlet Letter*. The main difference
between the two tales is the fact that in the American
story the husband plays an all-important part, and in
the Scottish plays almost none at all. *Adam Blair* is
the history of the passion, and *The Scarlet Letter* the
history of its sequel; but nevertheless, if one has read
the two books at a short interval, it is impossible to
avoid confronting them. I confess that a large portion
of the interest of *Adam Blair*, to my mind, when once
I had perceived that it would repeat in a great measure
the situation of *The Scarlet Letter*, lay in noting its
difference of tone. It threw into relief the passionless
quality of Hawthorne's novel, its element of cold and
ingenious fantasy, its elaborate imaginative delicacy.
These things do not precisely constitute a weakness in
The Scarlet Letter ; indeed, in a certain way they constitute a great strength; but the absence of a certain
something warm and straightforward, a trifle more
grossly human and vulgarly natural, which one finds in
Adam Blair, will always make Hawthorne's tale less
touching to a large number of even very intelligent
readers, than a love-story told with the robust, synthetic
pathos which served Lockhart so well. His novel is
not of the first rank (I should call it an excellent

second-rate one), but it borrows a charm from the fact
that his vigorous, but not strongly imaginative, mind
was impregnated with the reality of his subject. He
did not always succeed in rendering this reality; the
expression is sometimes awkward and poor. But the
reader feels that his vision was clear, and his feeling
about the matter very strong and rich. Hawthorne's
imagination, on the other hand, plays with his theme
so incessantly, leads it such a dance through the moon-
lighted air of his intellect, that the thing cools off, as
it were, hardens and stiffens, and, producing effects
much more exquisite, leaves the reader with a sense of
having handled a splendid piece of silversmith's work.
Lockhart, by means much more vulgar, produces at
moments a greater illusion, and satisfies our inevitable desire for something, in the people in whom it is
sought to interest us, that shall be of the same pitch
and the same continuity with ourselves. Above all,
it is interesting to see how the same subject appears
to two men of a thoroughly different cast of mind and
of a different race. Lockhart was struck with the
warmth of the subject that offered itself to him, and
Hawthorne with its coldness; the one with its glow,
its sentimental interest—the other with its shadow,
its moral interest. Lockhart's story is as decent, as
severely draped, as *The Scarlet Letter;* but the author
has a more vivid sense than appears to have imposed
itself upon Hawthorne, of some of the incidents of the
situation he describes; his tempted man and tempting
woman are more actual and personal; his heroine in
especial, though not in the least a delicate or a subtle
conception, has a sort of credible, visible, palpable property, a vulgar roundness and relief, which are lacking

to the dim and chastened image of Hester Prynne.
But I am going too far; I am comparing simplicity
with subtlety, the usual with the refined. Each man
wrote as his turn of mind impelled him, but each
expressed something more than himself. Lockhart was
a dense, substantial Briton, with a taste for the concrete, and Hawthorne was a thin New Englander, with
a miasmatic conscience.

In *The Scarlet Letter* there is a great deal of symbolism; there is, I think, too much. It is overdone at
times, and becomes mechanical; it ceases to be impressive, and grazes triviality. The idea of the mystic
A which the young minister finds imprinted upon his
breast and eating into his flesh, in sympathy with the
embroidered badge that Hester is condemned to wear,
appears to me to be a case in point. This suggestion
should, I think, have been just made and dropped; to
insist upon it and return to it, is to exaggerate the
weak side of the subject. Hawthorne returns to it
constantly, plays with it, and seems charmed by it;
until at last the reader feels tempted to declare that his
enjoyment of it is puerile. In the admirable scene, so
superbly conceived and beautifully executed, in which
Mr. Dimmesdale, in the stillness of the night, in the
middle of the sleeping town, feels impelled to go and
stand upon the scaffold where his mistress had formerly
enacted her dreadful penance, and then, seeing Hester
pass along the street, from watching at a sick-bed, with
little Pearl at her side, calls them both to come and
stand there beside him—in this masterly episode the
effect is almost spoiled by the introduction of one of
these superficial conceits. What leads up to it is very
fine—so fine that I cannot do better than quote it

as a specimen of one of the striking pages of the book.

"But before Mr. Dimmesdale had done speaking, a light gleamed far and wide over all the muffled sky. It was doubtless caused by one of those meteors which the night-watcher may so often observe burning out to waste in the vacant regions of the atmosphere. So powerful was its radiance that it thoroughly illuminated the dense medium of cloud, betwixt the sky and earth. The great vault brightened, like the dome of an immense lamp. It showed the familiar scene of the street with the distinctness of mid-day, but also with the awfulness that is always imparted to familiar objects by an unaccustomed light. The wooden houses, with their jutting stories and quaint gable-peaks ; the doorsteps and thresholds, with the early grass springing up about them ; the garden-plots, black with freshly-turned earth ; the wheel-track, little worn, and, even in the market-place, margined with green on either side ;—all were visible, but with a singularity of aspect that seemed to give another moral interpretation to the things of this world than they had ever borne before. And there stood the minister, with his hand over his heart ; and Hester Prynne, with the em-broidered letter glimmering on her bosom ; and little Pearl, herself a symbol, and the connecting-link between these two. They stood in the noon of that strange and solemn splendour, as if it were the light that is to reveal all secrets, and the daybreak that shall unite all that belong to one another."

That is imaginative, impressive, poetic ; but when, almost immediately afterwards, the author goes on to say that "the minister looking upward to the zenith, beheld there the appearance of an immense letter—the letter *A*—marked out in lines of dull red light," we feel that he goes too far and is in danger of crossing the line that separates the sublime from its intimate neighbour. We are tempted to say that this is not moral tragedy, but physical comedy. In the same way, too much is made of the intimation that Hester's badge had a scorching property, and that if one touched it one would immediately withdraw one's hand. Hawthorne is perpetually looking for images which shall place themselves in picturesque correspondence with the spiritual facts with which he is concerned, and of course the search is of the very essence of poetry. But in such a process discretion is everything, and when the image becomes importunate it is in danger of seeming to stand for nothing more serious than itself. When Hester meets the minister by appointment in the forest, and sits talking with him while little Pearl wanders away and plays by the edge of the brook, the child is represented as at last making her way over to the other side of the woodland stream, and disporting herself there in a manner which makes her mother feel herself. " in some indistinct and tantalising manner, estranged from Pearl; as if the child, in her lonely ramble through the forest, had strayed out of the sphere in which she and her mother dwelt together, and was now vainly seeking to return to it." And Hawthorne devotes a chapter to this idea of the child's having, by putting the brook between Hester and herself, established a kind of spiritual gulf, on the verge of which her little fantastic person innocently mocks at her mother's sense of bereavement. This conception belongs, one would say, quite to the lighter order of a story-teller's devices, and the reader hardly goes with Hawthorne in the large development he gives to it. He hardly goes with him either, I think, in his extreme predilection for a small number of vague ideas which are repre- sented by such terms as "sphere" and "sympathies."

Hawthorne, makes too liberal a use of these two sub-
stantives; it is the solitary defect of his style; and it
counts as a defect partly because the words in question
are a sort of specialty with certain writers immeasurably inferior to himself.

I had not meant, however, to expatiate upon his
defects, which are of the slenderest and most venial
kind. *The Scarlet Letter* has the beauty and harmony
of all original and complete conceptions, and its weaker
spots, whatever they are, are not of its essence; they
are mere light flaws and inequalities of surface. One
can often return to it; it supports familiarity and has
the inexhaustible charm and mystery of great works of
art. It is admirably written. Hawthorne afterwards
polished his style to a still higher degree, but in his
later productions—it is almost always the case in a
writer's later productions—there is a touch of mannerism.
In *The Scarlet Letter* there is a high degree of polish,
and at the same time a charming freshness; his phrase
is less conscious of itself. His biographer very justly
calls attention to the fact that his style was excellent
from the beginning; that he appeared to have passed
through no phase of learning how to write, but was in
possession of his means from the first of his handling
a pen. His early tales, perhaps, were not of a character
to subject his faculty of expression to a very severe test,
but a man who had not Hawthorne's natural sense of
language would certainly have contrived to write them
less well. This natural sense of language—this turn
for saying things lightly and yet touchingly, picturesquely yet simply, and for infusing a gently
colloquial tone into matter of the most unfamiliar
import, he had evidently cultivated with great assiduity.

I have spoken of the anomalous character of his Note-Books—of his going to such pains often to make a record of incidents which either were not worth remembering or could be easily remembered without its aid.   But it helps us to understand the Note-Books if we regard them as a literary exercise.   They were compositions, as school boys say, in which the subject was only the pretext, and the main point was to write a certain amount of excellent English.   Hawthorne must at least have written a great many of these things for practice, and he must often have said to himself that it was better practice to write about trifles, because it was a greater tax upon one's skill to make them interesting.   And his theory was just, for he has almost always made his trifles interesting.   In his novels his art of saying things well is very positively tested, for here he treats of those matters among which it is very easy for a blundering writer to go wrong—the subtleties and mysteries of life, the moral and spiritual maze.   In such a passage as one I have marked for quotation from *The Scarlet Letter* there is the stamp of the genius of style.

" Hester Prynne, gazing steadfastly at the clergyman, felt a dreary influence come over her, but wherefore or whence she knew not, unless that he seemed so remote from her own sphere and utterly beyond her reach.   One glance of recognition she had imagined must needs pass between them.   She thought of the dim forest with its little dell of solitude, and love, and anguish, and the mossy tree-trunk, where, sitting hand in hand, they had mingled their sad and passionate talk with the melancholy murmur of the brook.   How deeply had they known each other then !   And was this the man ?   She hardly knew him now !   He, moving proudly past, enveloped as it were in the rich music, with the procession of majestic and venerable fathers ; he, so unattainable in his worldly

position, and still more so in that far vista in his
unsympathising thoughts, through which she now beheld
him! Her spirit sank with the idea that all must have been
a delusion, and that vividly as she had dreamed it, there
could be no real bond betwixt the clergyman and herself.
And thus much of woman there was in Hester, that she
could scarcely forgive him—least of all now, when the heavy
footstep of their approaching fate might be heard, nearer,
nearer, nearer!—for being able to withdraw himself so completely from their mutual world, while she groped darkly,
and stretched forth her cold hands, and found him not!"

The House of the Seven Gables was written at Lenox,
among the mountains of Massachusetts, a village nest-
ling, rather loosely, in one of the loveliest corners of
New England, to which Hawthorne had betaken himself
after the success of *The Scarlet Letter* became conspicuous, in the summer of 1850, and where he occupied
for two years an uncomfortable little red house which is
now pointed out to the inquiring stranger. The inquiring
stranger is now a frequent figure at Lenox, for the
place has suffered the process of lionisation. It has
become a prosperous watering-place, or at least (as there
are no waters), as they say in America, a summer-resort.
It is a brilliant and generous landscape, and thirty years
ago a man of fancy, desiring to apply himself, might
have found both inspiration and tranquillity there.
Hawthorne found so much of both that he wrote more
during his two years of residence at Lenox than at any
period of his career. He began with *The House of the
Seven Gables*, which was finished in the early part of
1851. This is the longest of his three American novels,
it is the most elaborate, and in the judgment of some
persons it is the finest. It is a rich, delightful, imaginative work, larger and more various than its companions,

and full of all sorts of deep intentions, of interwoven threads of suggestion But it is not so rounded and complete as *The Scarlet Letter;* it has always seemed to me more like a prologue to a great novel than a great novel itself. I think this is partly owing to the fact that the subject, the *donnée*, as the French say, of the story, does not quite fill it out, and that we get at the same time an impression of certain complicated purposes on the author's part, which seem to reach beyond it. I call it larger and more various than its companions, and it has indeed a greater richness of tone and density of detail. The colour, so to speak, of *The House of the Seven Gables* is admirable. But the story has a sort of expansive quality which never wholly fructifies, and as I lately laid it down, after reading it for the third time, I had a sense of having interested myself in a magnificent fragment. Yet the book has a great fascination, and of all of those of its author's productions which I have read over while writing this sketch, it is perhaps the one that has gained most by re-perusal. If it be true of the others that the pure, natural quality of the imaginative strain is their great merit, this is at least as true of *The House of the Seven Gables*, the charm of which is in a peculiar degree of the kind that we fail to reduce to its grounds—like that of the sweetness of a piece of music, or the softness of fine September weather. It is vague, indefinable, ineffable ; but it is the sort of thing we must always point to in justification of the high claim that we make for Hawthorne. In this case of course its vagueness is a drawback, for it is difficult to point to ethereal beauties ; and if the reader whom we have wished to inoculate with our admiration inform us after looking a while that he perceives nothing in particular, we can only reply that, in effect, the object is a delicate one.

The House of the Seven Gables comes nearer being a picture of contemporary American life than either of its companions; but on this ground it would be a mistake to make a large claim for it. It cannot be too often repeated that Hawthorne was not a realist. He had a high sense of reality—his Note-Books superabundantly testify to it; and fond as he was of jotting down the items that make it up, he never attempted to render exactly or closely the actual facts of the society that surrounded him. I have said—I began by saying —that his pages were full of its spirit, and of a certain reflected light that springs from it; but I was careful to add that the reader must look for his local and national quality between the lines of his writing and in the *indirect* testimony of his tone, his accent, his temper, of his very omissions and suppressions. *The House of the Seven Gables* has, however, more literal actuality than the others, and if it were not too fanciful an account of it, I should say that it renders, to an initiated reader, the impression of a summer afternoon in an elm-shadowed New England town. It leaves upon the mind a vague correspondence to some such reminiscence, and in stirring up the association it renders it delightful. The comparison is to the honour of the New England town, which gains in it more than it bestows. The shadows of the elms, in *The House of the Seven Gables*, are exceptionally dense and cool; the summer afternoon is peculiarly still and beautiful; the atmosphere has a delicious warmth, and the long daylight seems to pause and rest. But the mild provincial quality is there, the mixture of shabbiness and freshness, the paucity of ingredients. The end of an old race—this is the situation that Hawthorne has depicted, and he has been admirably inspired in the choice of the figures in whom he seeks to interest us. They are all figures rather than characters—they are all pictures rather than persons. But if their reality is light and vague, it is sufficient, and it is in harmony with the low relief and dimness of outline of the objects that surround them. They are all types, to the author's mind, of something general, of something that is bound up with the history, at large, of families and individuals, and each of them is the centre of a cluster of those ingenious and meditative musings, rather melancholy, as a general thing, than joyous, which melt into the current and texture of the story and give it a kind of moral richness. A grotesque old spinster, simple, childish, penniless, very humble at heart, but rigidly conscious of her pedigree; an amiable bachelor, of an epicurean temperament and an enfeebled intellect, who has passed twenty years of his life in penal confinement for a crime of which he was unjustly pronounced guilty; a sweet-natured and bright-faced young girl from the country, a poor relation of these two ancient decrepitudes, with whose moral mustiness her modern freshness and soundness are contrasted; a young man still more modern, holding the latest opinions, who has sought his fortune up and down the world, and, though he has not found it, takes a genial and enthusiastic view of the future: these, with two or three remarkable accessory figures, are the persons concerned in the little drama. The drama is a small one, but as Hawthorne does not put it before us for its own superficial sake, for the dry facts of the case, but for something in it which he holds to be symbolic and of large application, something that points a moral and that it behoves us to remember, the scenes in the rusty wooden house whose gables give its name to the story, have something of the dignity both of history and of tragedy. Miss Hephzibah Pyncheon, dragging out a disappointed life in her paternal dwelling, finds herself obliged in her old age to open a little shop for the sale of penny toys and gingerbread. This is the central incident of the tale, and, as Hawthorne relates it, it is an incident of the most impressive magnitude and most touching interest. Her dishonoured and vague-minded brother is released from prison at the same moment, and returns to the ancestral roof to deepen her perplexities. But, on the other hand, to alleviate them, and to introduce a breath of the air of the outer world into this long unventilated interior, the little country cousin also arrives, and proves the good angel of the feebly distracted household. All this episode is exquisite—admirably conceived, and executed with a kind of humorous tenderness, an equal sense of everything in it that is picturesque, touching, ridiculous, worthy of the highest praise. Hephzibah Pyncheon, with her near-sighted scowl, her rusty joints, her antique turban, her map of a great territory to the eastward which ought to have belonged to her family, her vain terrors and scruples and resentments, the inaptitude and repugnance of an ancient gentlewoman to the vulgar little commerce which a cruel fate has compelled her to engage in—Hephzibah Pyncheon is a masterly picture. I repeat that she is a picture, as her companions are pictures; she is a charming piece of descriptive writing, rather than a dramatic exhibition. But she is described, like her companions too, so subtly

and lovingly that we enter into her virginal old heart
and stand with her behind her abominable little counter.
Clifford Pyncheon is a still more remarkable conception,
though he is perhaps not so vividly depicted. It was a
figure needing a much more subtle touch, however, and
it was of the essence of his character to be vague and
unemphasised. Nothing can be more charming than
the manner in which the soft, bright, active presence
of Phœbe Pyncheon is indicated, or than the account of
her relations with the poor dimly sentient kinsman for
whom her light-handed sisterly offices, in the evening of
a melancholy life, are a revelation of lost possibilities
of happiness. " In her aspect," Hawthorne says of the
young girl, " there was a familiar gladness, and a holi-
ness that you could play with, and yet reverence it as
much as ever. She was like a prayer offered up in the
homeliest beauty of one's mother-tongue. Fresh was
Phœbe, moreover, and airy, and sweet in her apparel ;
as if nothing that she wore—neither her gown, nor her
small straw bonnet, nor her little kerchief, any more
than her snowy stockings—had ever been put on before ;
or if worn, were all the fresher for it, and with a
fragrance as if they had lain among the rose-buds."
Of the influence of her maidenly salubrity upon poor
Clifford, Hawthorne gives the prettiest description, and
then, breaking off suddenly, renounces the attempt in
language which, while pleading its inadequacy, conveys
an exquisite satisfaction to the reader. I quote the
passage for the sake of its extreme felicity, and of the
charming image with which it concludes.

"But we strive in vain to put the idea into words. No
adequate expression of the beauty and profound pathos with
which it impresses us is attainable. This being, made only

for happiness, and heretofore so miserably failing 'to be
happy—his tendencies so hideously thwarted that some unknown time ago, the delicate springs of his character, never
morally or intellectually strong, had given way, and he was
now imbecile—this poor forlorn voyager from the Islands of
the Blest, in a frail bark, on a tempestuous sea, had been
flung by the last mountain-wave of his shipwreck, into a
quiet harbour. There, as he lay more than half lifeless on the
strand, the fragrance of an earthly rose-bud had come to his
nostrils, and, as odours will, had summoned up reminiscences
or visions of all the living and breathing beauty amid which
he should have had his home. With his native susceptibility
of happy influences, he inhales the slight ethereal rapture
into his soul, and expires ! "

I have not mentioned the personage in *The House of
the Seven Gables* upon whom Hawthorne evidently bestowed most pains, and whose portrait is the most
elaborate in the book ; partly because he is, in spite
of the space he occupies, an accessory figure, and partly
because, even more than the others, he is what I have
called a picture rather than a character. Judge Pyncheon is an ironical portrait, very richly and broadly
executed, very sagaciously composed and rendered—the
portrait of a superb, full-blown hypocrite, a large-based,
full-nurtured Pharisee, bland, urbane, impressive, dif-
fusing about him a " sultry " warmth of benevolence,
as the author calls it again and again, and basking in
the noontide of prosperity and the consideration of
society ; but in reality hard, gross, and ignoble. Judge
Pyncheon is an elaborate piece of description, made up
of a hundred admirable touches, in which satire is
always winged with fancy, and fancy is linked with a
deep sense of reality. It is difficult to say whether
Hawthorne followed a model in describing Judge

Pyncheon ; but it is tolerably obvious that the picture is
an impression—a copious impression—of an individual.
It has evidently a definite starting-point in fact, and
the author is able to draw, freely and confidently, after
the image established in his mind.   Holgrave, the
modern young man, who has been a Jack-of-all-trades
and is at the period of the story a daguerreotypist, is
an attempt to render a kind of national type—that of
the young citizen of the United States whose fortune is
simply in his lively intelligence, and who stands naked,
as it were, unbiased and unencumbered alike, in the
centre of the far-stretching level of American life.
Holgrave is intended as a contrast ; his lack of traditions, his democratic stamp, his condensed experience,
are opposed to the desiccated prejudices and exhausted
vitality of the race of which poor feebly-scowling, rusty-
jointed Hephzibah is the most heroic representative.
It is perhaps a pity that Hawthorne should not have
proposed to himself to give the old Pyncheon-qualities
some embodiment which would help them to balance
more fairly with the elastic properties of the young
daguerreotypist—should not have painted a lusty conservative to match his strenuous radical.   As it is, the
mustiness and mouldiness of the tenants of the House
of the Seven Gables crumble away rather too easily.
Evidently, however, what Hawthorne designed to represent was not the struggle between an old society
and a new, for in this case he would have given the old
one a better chance ; but simply, as I have said, the
shrinkage and extinction of a family.   This appealed
to his imagination ; and the idea of long perpetuation
and survival always appears to have filled him with a
kind of horror and disapproval.   Conservative, in a

K

certain degree, as he was himself, and fond of retrospect and quietude and the mellowing influences of
time, it is singular how often one encounters in his
writings some expression of mistrust of old houses, old
institutions, long lines of descent. He was disposed
apparently to allow a very moderate measure in these
respects, and he condemns the dwelling of the Pyncheons to disappear from the face of the earth because
it has been standing a couple of hundred years. In
this he was an American of Americans; or rather he
was more American than many of his countrymen, who,
though they are accustomed to work for the short run
rather than the long, have often a lurking esteem for
things that show the marks of having lasted. I will
add that Holgrave is one of the few figures, among
those which Hawthorne created, with regard to which
the absence of the realistic mode of treatment is felt as
a loss. Holgrave is not sharply enough characterised;
he lacks features; he is not an individual, but a type.
But my last word about this admirable novel must not
be a restrictive one. It is a large and generous production, pervaded with that vague hum, that indefinable
echo, of the whole multitudinous life of man, which is
the real sign of a great work of fiction.

After the publication of *The House of the Seven
Gables*, which brought him great honour, and, I believe,
a tolerable share of a more ponderable substance, he
composed a couple of little volumes for children—
The Wonder-Book, and a small collection of stories
entitled *Tanglewood Tales*. They are not among his
most serious literary titles, but if I may trust my own
early impression of them, they are among the most charming literary services that have been rendered to children

in an age (and especially in a country) in which the
exactions of the infant mind have exerted much too
palpable an influence upon literature. Hawthorne's
stories are the old Greek myths, made more vivid to
the childish imagination by an infusion of details which
both deepen and explain their marvels. I have been
careful not to read them over, for I should be very
sorry to risk disturbing in any degree a recollection of
them that has been at rest since the appreciative period
of life to which they are addressed. They seem at that
period enchanting, and the ideal of happiness of many
American children is to lie upon the carpet and lose
themselves in *The Wonder-Book*. It is in its pages that
they first make the acquaintance of the heroes and
heroines of the antique mythology, and something
of the nursery fairy-tale quality of interest which
Hawthorne imparts to them always remains.

I have said that Lenox was a very pretty place, and
that he was able to work there Hawthorne proved by
composing *The House of the Seven Gables* with a good
deal of rapidity. But at the close of the year in which
this novel was published he wrote to a friend (Mr.
Fields, his publisher,) that "to tell you a secret I am
sick to death of Berkshire, and hate to think of spending
another winter here. . . . . The air and climate do not
agree with my health at all, and for the first time since
I was a boy I have felt languid and dispirited. . . . .
O that Providence would build me the merest little
shanty, and mark me out a rood or two of garden
ground, near the sea-coast!" He was at this time for a
while out of health ; and it is proper to remember that
though the Massachusetts Berkshire, with its mountains
and lakes. was charming during the ardent American

summer, there was a reverse to the medal, consisting
of December snows prolonged into April and May.
Providence failed to provide him with a cottage by the
sea; but he betook himself for the winter of 1852 to
the little town of West Newton, near Boston, where he
brought into the world *The Blithedale Romance*.

This work, as I have said, would not have been
written if Hawthorne had not spent a year at Brook
Farm, and though it is in no sense of the word an
account of the manners or the inmates of that estab-
lishment, it will preserve the memory of the ingenious
community at West Roxbury for a generation unconscious of other reminders. I hardly know what to
say about it save that it is very charming ; this vague,
unanalytic epithet is the first that comes to one's pen
in treating of Hawthorne's novels, for their extreme
amenity of form invariably suggests it ; but if on the
one hand it claims to be uttered, on the other it frankly
confesses its inconclusiveness. Perhaps, however, in
this case, it fills out the measure of appreciation
more completely than in others, for *The Blithedale
Romance* is the lightest, the brightest, the liveliest,
of this company of unhumorous fictions.

The story is told from a more joyous point of view—
from a point of view comparatively humorous—and a
number of objects and incidents touched with the light
of the profane world—the vulgar, many-coloured world
of actuality, as distinguished from the crepuscular
realm of the writer's own reveries—are mingled with its
course. The book indeed is a mixture of elements,
and it leaves in the memory an impression analogous to
that of an April day—an alternation of brightness and
shadow, of broken sun-patches and sprinkling clouds.

Its dénoûment is tragical—there is indeed nothing so
tragical in all Hawthorne, unless it be the murder of
Miriam's persecutor by Donatello, in *Transformation*,
as the suicide of Zenobia; and yet on the whole the
effect of the novel is to make one think more agreeably
of life. The standpoint of the narrator has the advantage of being a concrete one; he is no longer, as in the
preceding tales, a disembodied spirit, imprisoned in the
haunted chamber of his own contemplations, but a
particular man, with a certain human grossness.

Of Miles Coverdale I have already spoken, and of its
being natural to assume that in so far as we may measure this lightly indicated identity of his, it has a great
deal in common with that of his creator. Coverdale
is a picture of the contemplative, observant, analytic
nature, nursing its fancies, and yet, thanks to an
element of strong good sense, not bringing them up to
be spoiled children; having little at stake in life, at any
given moment, and yet indulging, in imagination, in a
good many adventures; a portrait of a man, in a word,
whose passions are slender, whose imagination is active,
and whose happiness lies, not in doing, but in perceiving—half a poet, half a critic, and all a spectator.
He is contrasted, excellently, with the figure of
Hollingsworth, the heavily treading Reformer, whose
attitude with regard to the world is that of the hammer
to the anvil, and who has no patience with his friend's
indifferences and neutralities. Coverdale is a gentle
sceptic, a mild cynic; he would agree that life is a little
worth living—or worth living a little; but would
remark that, unfortunately, to live little enough, we
have to live a great deal. He confesses to a want of
earnestness, but in reality he is evidently an excellent

fellow, to whom one might look, not for any personal
performance on a great scale, but for a good deal of
generosity of detail. " As Hollingsworth once told me,
I lack a purpose," he writes, at the close of his story.
" How strange ! He was ruined, morally, by an over-
plus of the same ingredient the want of which, I
occasionally suspect, has rendered my own life all an
emptiness. I by no means wish to die. Yet were
there any cause in this whole chaos of human struggle,
worth a sane man's dying for, and which my death
would benefit, then—provided, however, the effort did
not involve an unreasonable amount of trouble—
methinks I might be bold to offer up my life. If
Kossuth, for example, would pitch the battle-field of
Hungarian rights within an easy ride of my abode, and
choose a mild sunny morning, after breakfast, for the
conflict, Miles Coverdale would gladly be his man, for
one brave rush upon the levelled bayonets. Further
than that I should be loth to pledge myself."

The finest thing in *The Blithdale Romance* is the character of Zenobia, which I have said elsewhere strikes
me as the nearest approach that Hawthorne has made
to the complete creation of a *person*. She is more
concrete than Hester or Miriam, or Hilda or Phœbe ;
she is a more definite image, produced by a greater
multiplicity of touches. It is idle to inquire too closely
whether Hawthorne had Margaret Fuller in his mind
in constructing the figure of this brilliant specimen of
the strong-minded class and endowing her with the
genius of conversation ; or, on the assumption that such
was the case, to compare the image at all strictly with
the model. There is no strictness in the representation
by novelists of persons who have struck them in life,

and there can in the nature of things be none. From
the moment the imagination takes a hand in the game,
the inevitable tendency is to divergence, to following
what may be called new scents. The original gives
hints, but the writer does what he likes with them, and
imports new elements into the picture. If there is this
amount of reason for referring the wayward heroine of
Blithedale to Hawthorne's impression of the most distinguished woman of her day in Boston, that Margaret
Fuller was the only literary lady of eminence whom
there is any sign of his having known, that she was
proud, passionate, and eloquent, that she was much
connected with the little world of Transcendentalism
out of which the experiment of Brook Farm sprung,
and that she had a miserable end and a watery grave—
if these are facts to be noted on one side, I say ; on the
other, the beautiful and sumptuous Zenobia, with her
rich and picturesque temperament and physical aspects,
offers many points of divergence from the plain and
strenuous invalid who represented feminine culture in
the suburbs of the New England metropolis.   This picturesqueness of Zenobia is very happily indicated and
maintained ; she is a woman, in all the force of the
term, and there is something very vivid and powerful in
her large expression of womanly gifts and weaknesses.
Hollingsworth is, I think, less successful, though there
is much reality in the conception of the type to which
he belongs—the strong-willed, narrow-hearted apostle of
a special form of redemption for society.   There is
nothing better in all Hawthorne than the scene
between him and Coverdale, when the two men are
at work together in the field (piling stones on a dyke),
and he gives it to his companion to choose whether he

will be with him or against him. It is a pity, perhaps, to have represented him as having begun life as a blacksmith, for one grudges him the advantage of so logical a reason for his roughness and hardness.

" Hollingsworth scarcely said a word, unless when repeatedly and pertinaciously addressed. Then indeed he would glare upon us from the thick shrubbery of his meditations, like a tiger out of a jungle, make the briefest reply possible, and betake himself back into the solitude of his heart and mind . . . . His heart, I imagine, was never really interested in our socialist scheme, but was for ever busy with his strange, and as most people thought, impracticable plan for the reformation of criminals through an appeal to their higher instincts. Much as I liked Hollingsworth, it cost me many a groan to tolerate him on this point. He ought to have commenced his investigation of the subject by committing some huge sin in his proper person, and examining the condition of his higher instincts afterwards."

The most touching element in the novel is the history of the grasp that this barbarous fanatic has laid upon the fastidious and high-tempered Zenobia, who, disliking him and shrinking from him at a hundred points, is drawn into the gulf of his omnivorous egotism. The portion of the story that strikes me as least felicitous is that which deals with Priscilla and with her mysterious relation to Zenobia—with her mesmeric gifts, her clairvoyance, her identity with the Veiled Lady, her divided subjection to Hollingsworth and Westervelt, and her numerous other graceful but fantastic properties — her Sibylline attributes, as the author calls them. Hawthorne is rather too fond of Sibylline attributes—a taste of the same order as his disposition, to which I have already alluded, to talk about spheres and sympathies. As the action advances,

in *The Blithdale Romance*, we get too much out of
reality, and cease to feel beneath our feet the firm
ground of an appeal to our own vision of the world, our
observation.   I should have liked to see the story concern itself more with the little community in which its
earlier scenes are laid, and avail itself of so excellent an
opportunity for describing unhackneyed specimens of
human nature.   I have already spoken of the absence of
satire in the novel, of its not aiming in the least at
satire, and of its offering no grounds for complaint as
an invidious picture.   Indeed the brethren of Brook
Farm should have. held themselves slighted rather than
misrepresented, and have regretted that the admirable
genius who for a while was numbered among them
should have treated their institution mainly as a perch
for starting upon an imaginative flight.   But when all
is said about a certain want of substance and cohesion
in the latter portions of *The Blithedale Romance*, the
book is still a delightful and beautiful one.   Zenobia
and Hollingsworth live in the memory, and even Priscilla and Coverdale, who linger there less importunately,
have a great deal that touches us and that we believe
in.   I said just now that Priscilla was infelicitous ; but
immediately afterwards I open the volume at a page
in which the author describes some of the out-of-door
amusements at Blithedale, and speaks of a foot-race
across the grass, in which some of the slim young girls
of the society joined.   "Priscilla's peculiar charm in a
foot-race was the weakness and irregularity with which
she ran.   Growing up without exercise, except to her
poor little fingers, she had never yet acquired the perfect use of her legs.   Setting buoyantly forth therefore,
as if no rival less swift than Atalanta could compete

with her, she ran falteringly, and often tumbled on the grass. Such an incident—though it seems too slight to think of—was a thing to laugh at, but which brought the water into one's eyes, and lingered in the memory after far greater joys and sorrows were wept out of it, as antiquated trash. Priscilla's life, as I beheld it, was full of trifles that affected me in just this way." That seems to me exquisite, and the book is full of touches as deep and delicate.

After writing it, Hawthorne went back to live in Concord, where he had bought a small house in which, apparently, he expected to spend a large portion of his future. This was in fact the dwelling in which he passed that part of the rest of his days that he spent in his own country. He established himself there before going to Europe, in 1853, and he returned to the Wayside, as he called his house, on coming back to the United States seven years later. Though he actually occupied the place no long time, he had made it his property, and it was more his own home than any of his numerous provisional abodes. I may therefore quote a little account of the house which he wrote to a distinguished friend, Mr. George Curtis.

"As for my old house, you will understand it better after spending a day or two in it. Before Mr. Alcott took it in hand, it was a mean-looking affair, with two peaked gables; no suggestiveness about it, and no venerableness, although from the style of its construction it seems to have survived beyond its first century. He added a porch in front, and a central peak, and a piazza at each end, and painted it a rusty olive hue, and invested the whole with a modest picturesqueness; all which improvements, together with its situation at the foot of a wooded hill, make it a place that one notices and remembers for a few moments after passing. Mr. Alcott

expended a good deal of taste and some money (to no great
purpose) in forming the hillside behind the house into
terraces, and building arbours and summer-houses of rough
stems and branches and trees, on a system of his own. They
must have been very pretty in their day, and are so still,
although much decayed, and shattered more and more by
every breeze that blows. The hillside is covered chiefly with
locust trees, which come into luxuriant blossom in the month
of June, and look and smell very sweetly, intermixed with a
few young elms, and white pines and infant oaks — the
whole forming rather a thicket than a wood. Nevertheless,
there is some very good shade to be found there. I spend
delectable hours there in the hottest part of the day, stretched
out at my lazy length, with a book in my hand, or some
unwritten book in my thoughts. There is almost always a
breeze stirring along the sides or brow of the hill. From the
hill-top there is a good view along the extensive level sur-
faces and gentle hilly outlines, covered with wood, that
characterise the scenery of Concord. . . . . I know nothing
of the history of the house except Thoreau's telling me that
it was inhabited, a generation or two ago, by a man who
believed he should never die. I believe, however, he is dead ;
at least, I hope so ; else he may probably reappear and
dispute my title to his residence."

As Mr. Lathrop points out, this allusion to a man
who believed he should never die is "the first intimation
of the story of *Septimius Felton*." The scenery of that
romance, he adds, "was evidently taken from the
Wayside and its hill." *Septimius Felton* is in fact a
young man who, at the time of the war of the Revolution, lives in the village of Concord, on the Boston road,
at the base of a woody hill which rises abruptly
behind his house, and of which the level summit
supplies him with a promenade continually mentioned
in the course of the tale. Hawthorne used to exercise

himself upon this picturesque eminence, and, as he conceived the brooding Septimius to have done before him, to betake himself thither when he found the limits of his dwelling too narrow. But he had an advantage which his imaginary hero lacked; he erected a tower as an adjunct to the house, and it was a jocular tradition among his neighbours, in allusion to his attributive tendency to evade rather than hasten the coming guest, that he used to ascend this structure and scan the road for provocations to retreat.

In so far, however, as Hawthorne suffered the penalties of celebrity at the hands of intrusive fellow-citizens, he was soon to escape from this honourable incommodity. On the 4th of March, 1853, his old college-mate and intimate friend, Franklin Pierce, was installed as President of the United States. He had been the candidate of the Democratic party, and all good Democrats, accordingly, in conformity to the beautiful and rational system under which the affairs of the great Republic were carried on, begun to open their windows to the golden sunshine of Presidential patronage. When General Pierce was put forward by the Democrats, Hawthorne felt a perfectly loyal and natural desire that his good friend should be exalted to so brilliant a position, and he did what was in him to further the good cause, by writing a little book about its hero. His *Life of Franklin Pierce* belongs to that class of literature which is known as the " campaign biography," and which consists of an attempt, more or less successful, to persuade the many-headed monster of universal suffrage that the gentleman on whose behalf it is addressed is a paragon of wisdom and virtue. Of Hawthorne's little book there is nothing particular

to say, save that it is in very good taste, that he is a
very fairly ingenious advocate, and that if he claimed
for the future President qualities which rather faded in
the bright light of a high office, this defect of proportion
was essential to his undertaking. He dwelt chiefly upon
General Pierce's exploits in the war with Mexico (before
that, his record, as they say in America, had been
mainly that of a successful country lawyer), and
exercised his descriptive powers so far as was possible in
describing the advance of the United States troops from
Vera Cruz to the city of the Montezumas. The mouth-
pieces of the Whig party spared him, I believe, no repro-
bation for " prostituting " his exquisite genius ; but I
fail to see anything reprehensible in Hawthorne's lend-
ing his old friend the assistance of his graceful quill.
He wished him to be President—he held afterwards
that he filled the office with admirable dignity and
wisdom—-and as the only thing he could do was to write,
he fell to work and wrote for him. Hawthorne was
a good lover and a very sufficient partisan, and I suspect
that if Franklin Pierce had been made even less of the
stuff of a statesman, he would still have found in the
force of old associations an injunction to hail him as a
ruler. Our hero was an American of the earlier and
simpler type—the type of which it is doubtless premature
to say that it has wholly passed away, but of which it
may at least be said that the circumstances that produced it have been greatly modified. The generation to
which he belonged, that generation which grew up with
the century, witnessed during a period of fifty years the
immense, uninterrupted material development of the
young Republic ; and when one thinks of the scale on

which it took place, of the prosperity that walked in its
train and waited on its course, of the hopes it fostered
and the blessings it conferred, of the broad morning
sunshine, in a word, in which it all went forward, there
seems to be little room for surprise that it should have
implanted a kind of superstitious faith in the grandeur
of the country, its duration, its immunity from the
usual troubles of earthly empires. This faith was a
simple and uncritical one, enlivened with an element of
genial optimism, in the light of which it appeared that
the great American state was not as other human institutions are, that a special Providence watched over it,
that it would go on joyously for ever, and that a country
whose vast and blooming bosom offered a refuge to the
strugglers and seekers of all the rest of the world, must
come off easily, in the battle of the ages. From this
conception of the American future the sense of its
having problems to solve was blissfully absent ; there
were no difficulties in the programme, no looming com-
plications, no rocks ahead. The indefinite multiplication
of the population, and its enjoyment of the benefits of
a common-school education and of unusual facilities for
making an income—this was the form in which, on the
whole, the future most vividly presented itself, and in
which the greatness of the country was to be recognised
of men. There was indeed a faint shadow in the picture
—the shadow projected by the " peculiar institution "
of the Southern States ; but it was far from sufficient
to darken the rosy vision of most good Americans, and
above all, of most good Democrats. Hawthorne alludes
to it in a passage of his life of Pierce, which I will
quote not only as a hint of the trouble that was in

store for a cheerful race of men, but as an example of
his own easy-going political attitude.

" It was while in the lower house of Congress that Franklin
Pierce took that stand on the Slavery question from which he
has never since swerved by a hair's breadth. He fully recognised by his votes and his voice, the rights pledged to the
South by the Constitution. This, at the period when he
declared himself, was an easy thing to do. But when it
became more difficult, when the first imperceptible murmur of
agitation had grown almost to a convulsion, his course was
still the same. Nor did he ever shun the obloquy that
sometimes threatened to pursue the Northern man who
dared to love that great and sacred reality—his whole united
country—better than the mistiness of a philanthropic
theory."

This last invidious allusion is to the disposition, not
infrequent at the North, but by no means general, to
set a decisive limit to further legislation in favour of the
cherished idiosyncrasy of the other half of the country.
Hawthorne takes the license of a sympathetic biographer
in speaking of his hero's having incurred obloquy by
his conservative attitude on the question of Slavery.
The only class in the American world that suffered in
the smallest degree, at this time, from social persecution, was the little band of Northern Abolitionists,
who were as unfashionable as they were indiscreet—
which is saying much. Like most of his fellow-country-
men, Hawthorne had no idea that the respectable
institution which he contemplated in impressive
contrast to humanitarian "mistiness," was presently to
cost the nation four long years of bloodshed and
misery, and a social revolution as complete as any the
world has seen. When this event occurred, he was

therefore proportionately horrified and depressed by it; it cut from beneath his feet the familiar ground which had long felt so firm, substituting a heaving and quaking medium in which his spirit found no rest. Such was the bewildered sensation of that earlier and simpler generation of which I have spoken; their illusions were rudely dispelled, and they saw the best of all possible republics given over to fratricidal carnage. This affair had no place in their scheme, and nothing was left for them but to hang their heads and close their eyes. The subsidence of that great convulsion has left a different tone from the tone it found, and one may say that the Civil War marks an era in the history of the American mind. It introduced into the national consciousness a certain sense of proportion and relation, of the world being a more complicated place than it had hitherto seemed, the future more treacherous, success more difficult. At the rate at which things are going, it is obvious that good Americans will be more numerous than ever; but the good American, in days to come, will be a more critical person than his complacent and confident grandfather. He has eaten of the tree of knowledge. He will not, I think, be a sceptic, and still less, of course, a cynic; but he will be, without discredit to his well-known capacity for action, an observer. He will remember that the ways of the Lord are inscrutable, and that this is a world in which everything happens; and eventualities, as the late Emperor of the French used to say, will not find him intellectually unprepared. The good American of which Hawthorne was so admirable a specimen was not critical, and it was perhaps for this reason that Franklin Pierce seemed to him a very proper President.

The least that General Pierce could do in exchange for so liberal a confidence was to offer his old friend one of the numerous places in his gift. Hawthorne had a great desire to go abroad and see something of the world, so that a consulate seemed the proper thing. He never stirred in the matter himself, but his friends strongly urged that something should be done ; and when he accepted the post of consul at Liverpool there was not a word of reasonable criticism to be offered on the matter. If General Pierce, who was before all things good-natured and obliging, had been guilty of no greater indiscretion than to confer this modest distinction upon the most honourable and discreet of men of letters, he would have made a more brilliant mark in the annals of American statesmanship. Liverpool had not been immediately selected, and Hawthorne had written to his friend and publisher, Mr. Fields, with some humorous vagueness of allusion to his probable expatriation.

" Do make some inquiries about Portugal ; as, for instance, in what part of the world it lies, and whether it is an empire, a kingdom, or a republic. Also, and more particularly, the expenses of living there, and whether the Minister would be likely to be much pestered with his own countrymen. Also, any other information about foreign countries would be acceptable to an inquiring mind."

It would seem from this that there had been a question of offering him a small diplomatic post ; but the emoluments of the place were justly taken into account, and it is to be supposed that those of the consulate at Liverpool were at least as great as the salary of the American

L

representative at Lisbon. Unfortunately, just after Hawthorne had taken possession of the former post, the salary attached to it was reduced by Congress, in an economical hour, to less than half the sum enjoyed by his predecessors. It was fixed at 7,500 dollars (£1,500); but the consular fees, which were often copious, were an added resource. At midsummer then. in 1853, Hawthorne was established in England.

CHAPTER VI.

ENGLAND AND ITALY.

HAWTHORNE was close upon fifty years of age when he came to Europe—a fact that should be remembered when those impressions which he recorded in five substantial volumes (exclusive of the novel written in Italy), occasionally affect us by the rigidity of their point of view. His Note-Books, kept during his residence in England, his two winters in Rome, his summer in Florence, were published after his death; his impressions of England, sifted, revised, and addressed directly to the public, he gave to the world shortly before this event. The tone of his European Diaries is often so fresh and unsophisticated that we find ourselves thinking of the writer as a young man, and it is only a certain final sense of something reflective and a trifle melancholy that reminds us that the simplicity which is on the whole the leading characteristic of their pages, is, though the simplicity of inexperience, not that of youth. When I say inexperience, I mean that Hawthorne's experience had been narrow. His fifty years had been spent, for much the larger part, in small American towns—Salem, the Boston of forty years ago, Concord, Lenox, West Newton—and he had led exclusively what one may call a

L 2

village-life. This is evident, not at all directly and superficially, but by implication and between the lines, in his desultory history of his foreign years. In other words, and to call things by their names, he was exquisitely and consistently provincial. I suggest this fact not in the least in condemnation, but, on the contrary, in support of an appreciative view of him. I know nothing more remarkable, more touching, than the sight of this odd, youthful-elderly mind, contending so late in the day with new opportunities for learning old things, and on the whole profiting by them so freely and gracefully. The Note-Books are provincial, and so, in a greatly modified degree, are the sketches of England, in *Our Old Home ;* but the beauty and delicacy of this latter work are so interwoven with the author's air of being remotely outside of everything he describes, that they count for more, seem more themselves, and finally give the whole thing the appearance of a triumph, not of initiation, but of the provincial point of view itself.

I shall not attempt to relate in detail the incidents of his residence in England. He appears to have enjoyed it greatly, in spite of the deficiency of charm in the place to which his duties chiefly confined him. His confinement, however, was not unbroken, and his published journals consist largely of minute accounts of little journeys and wanderings, with his wife and his three children, through the rest of the country ; together with much mention of numerous visits to London, a city for whose dusky immensity and multitudinous interest he professed the highest relish. His Note-Books are of the same cast as the two volumes of his American Diaries, of which I have given some account—chiefly occupied with external matters, with the accidents of

daily life, with observations made during the long
walks (often with his son), which formed his most
valued pastime. His office, moreover, though Liverpool
was not a delectable home, furnished him with entertainment as well as occupation, and it may almost be
said that during these years he saw more of his fellow-
countrymen, in the shape of odd wanderers, petitioners,
and inquirers of every kind, than he had ever done in
his native land. The paper entitled "Consular Experiences," in *Our Old Home*, is an admirable recital of
these observations, and a proof that the novelist might
have found much material in the opportunities of the
consul. On his return to America, in 1860, he drew
from his journal a number of pages relating to his
observations in England, re-wrote them (with, I should
suppose, a good deal of care), and converted them into
articles which he published in a magazine. These
chapters were afterwards collected, and *Our Old Home*
(a rather infelicitous title), was issued in 1863. I
prefer to speak of the book now, however, rather than
in touching upon the closing years of his life, for it is
a kind of deliberate *résumé* of his impressions of the
land of his ancestors. "It is not a good or a weighty
book," he wrote to his publisher, who had sent him
some reviews of it, "nor does it deserve any great
amount of praise or censure. I don't care about seeing
any more notices of it." Hawthorne's appreciation of
his own productions was always extremely just; he had
a sense of the relations of things, which some of his
admirers have not thought it well to cultivate; and
he never exaggerated his own importance as a writer.
Our Old Home is not a weighty book; it is decidedly a
light one. But when he says it is not a good one, I

hardly know what he means, and his modesty at this
point is in excess of his discretion. Whether good or
not, *Our Old Home* is charming—it is most delectable
reading.   The execution is singularly perfect and
ripe ; of all his productions it seems to be the best
written.   The touch, as musicians say, is admirable ;
the lightness, the fineness, the felicity of characterisation and description, belong to a man who has the
advantage of feeling delicately.   His judgment is by
no means always sound ; it often rests on too narrow
an observation.   But his perception is of the keenest,
and though it is frequently partial, incomplete, it is
excellent as far as it goes.   The book gave but limited
satisfaction, I believe, in England, and I am not sure
that the failure to enjoy certain manifestations of its
sportive irony, has not chilled the appreciation of its
singular grace.   That English readers, on the whole,
should have felt that Hawthorne did the national mind
and manners but partial justice, is, I think, conceivable ;
at the same time that it seems to me remarkable that the
tender side of the book, as I may call it, should not
have carried it off better.   It abounds in passages more
delicately appreciative than can easily be found elsewhere, and it contains more charming and affectionate
things than, I should suppose, had ever before been
written about a country not the writer's own.   To say
that it is an immeasurably more exquisite and sympathetic work than any of the numerous persons who have
related their misadventures in the United States have
seen fit to devote to that country, is to say but little,
and I imagine that Hawthorne had in mind the array of
English voyagers—Mrs. Trollope, Dickens, Marryat,
Basil Hall, Miss Martineau, Mr. Grattan—when he

reflected that everything is relative and that, as such
books go, his own little volume observed the amenities of
criticism. He certainly had it in mind when he wrote
the phrase in his preface relating to the impression the
book might make in England. "Not an Englishman
of them all ever spared America for courtesy's sake or
kindness; nor, in my opinion, would it contribute in
the least to any mutual advantage and comfort if we
were to besmear each other all over with butter and
honey." I am far from intending to intimate that the
vulgar instinct of recrimination had anything to do with
the restrictive passages of *Our Old Home;* I mean
simply that the author had a prevision that his collection of sketches would in some particulars fail to please
his English friends. He professed, after the event, to
have discovered that the English are sensitive, and as
they say of the Americans, for whose advantage I
believe the term was invented, thin-skinned. "The
English critics," he wrote to his publisher, "seem to
think me very bitter against their countrymen, and it is
perhaps natural that they should, because their self-
conceit can accept nothing short of indiscriminate
adulation; but I really think that Americans have much
more cause than they to complain of me. Looking over
the volume I am rather surprised to find that whenever
I draw a comparison between the two people, I almost
invariably cast the balance against ourselves." And he
writes at another time:—"I received several private
letters and printed notices of *Our Old Home* from
England. It is laughable to see the innocent wonder
with which they regard my criticisms, accounting for
them by jaundice, insanity, jealousy, hatred, on my part,
and never admitting the least suspicion that there may

be a particle of truth in them. The monstrosity of their self-conceit is such that anything short of unlimited admiration impresses them as malicious caricature. But they do me great injustice in supposing that I hate them. I would as soon hate my own people." The idea of his hating the English was of course too puerile for discussion ; and the book, as I have said, is full of a rich appreciation of the finest characteristics of the country. But it has a serious defect—a defect which impairs its value, though it helps to give consistency to such an image of Hawthorne's personal nature as we may by this time have been able to form. It is the work of an outsider, of a stranger, of a man who remains to the end a mere spectator (something less even than an observer), and always lacks the final initiation into the manners and nature of a people of whom it may most be said, among all the people of the earth, that to know them is to make discoveries. Hawthorne freely confesses to this constant exteriority, and appears to have been perfectly conscious of it. " I remember," he writes in the sketch of "A London Suburb," in *Our Old Home*, " I remember to this day the dreary feeling with which I sat by our first English fireside and watched the chill and rainy twilight of an autumn day darkening down upon the garden, while the preceding occupant of the house (evidently a most unamiable personage in his lifetime), scowled inhospitably from above the mantel-piece, as if indignant that an American should try to make himself at home there. Possibly it may appease his sulky shade to know that I quitted his abode as much a stranger as I entered it." The same note is struck in an entry in his journal, of the date of October 6th, 1854.

" The people, for several days, have been in the utmost
anxiety, and latterly in the highest exultation, about Sebas-
topol—and all England, and Europe to boot, have been
fooled by the belief that it had fallen. This, however, now
turns out to be incorrect; and the public visage is somewhat
grim in consequence. I am glad of it. In spite of his
actual sympathies, it is impossible for an American to be
otherwise than glad. Success makes an Englishman intoler-
able, and already, on the mistaken idea that the way was open
to a prosperous conclusion of the war, the *Times* had begun
to throw out menaces against America. I shall never love
England till she sues to us for help, and, in the meantime, the
fewer triumphs she obtains, the better for all parties. An
Englishman in adversity is a very respectable character; he
does not lose his dignity, but merely comes to a proper conception of himself. . . . . I seem to myself like a spy or
traitor when I meet their eyes, and am conscious that I
neither hope nor fear in sympathy with them, although they
look at me in full confidence of sympathy. Their heart
' knoweth its own bitterness,' and as for me, being a stranger
and an alien, I ' intermeddle not with their joy.' "

This seems to me to express very well the weak side
of Hawthorne's work—his constant mistrust and suspicion of the society that surrounded him, his exaggerated, painful, morbid national consciousness. It is,
I think, an indisputable fact that Americans are, as
Americans, the most self-conscious people in the world,
and the most addicted to the belief that the other
nations of the earth are in a conspiracy to undervalue
them. They are conscious of being the youngest of the
great nations, of not being of the European family, of
being placed on the circumference of the circle of civilisation rather than at the centre, of the experimental
element not having as yet entirely dropped out of their
great political undertaking. The sense of this relativity,

in a word, replaces that quiet and comfortable sense
of the absolute, as regards its own position in the
world, which reigns supreme in the British and in the
Gallic genius. Few persons, I think, can have mingled
much with Americans in Europe without having made
this reflection, and it is in England that their habit of
looking askance at foreign institutions—of keeping one
eye, as it were, on the American personality, while with
the other they contemplate these objects—is most to be
observed. Add to this that Hawthorne came to England late in life, when his habits, his tastes, his opinions,
were already formed, that he was inclined to look at
things in silence and brood over them gently, rather than
talk about them, discuss them, grow acquainted with
them by action ; and it will be possible to form an idea
of our writer's detached and critical attitude in the
country in which it is easiest, thanks to its aristocratic
constitution, to the absence of any considerable public
fund of entertainment and diversion, to the degree in
which the inexhaustible beauty and interest of the
place are private property, demanding constantly a
special introduction—in the country in which, I say, it is
easiest for a stranger to remain a stranger. For a
stranger to cease to be a stranger he must stand ready,
as the French say, to pay with his person ; and this was
an obligation that Hawthorne was indisposed to incur.
Our sense, as we read, that his reflections are those
of a shy and susceptible man, with nothing at stake,
mentally, in his appreciation of the country, is therefore a drawback to our confidence ; but it is not a
drawback sufficient to make it of no importance that he
is at the same time singularly intelligent and discrimi-
nating, with a faculty of feeling delicately and justly,

which constitutes in itself an illumination. There is a passage in the sketch entitled *About Warwick* which is a very good instance of what was probably his usual state of mind. He is speaking of the aspect of the High Street of the town.

"The street is an emblem of England itself. What seems new in it is chiefly a skilful and fortunate adaptation of what such a people as ourselves would destroy. The new things are based and supported on sturdy old things, and derive a massive strength from their deep and immemorial foundations, though with such limitations and impediments as only an Englishman could endure. But he likes to feel the weight of all the past upon his back ; and moreover the antiquity that overburdens him has taken root in his being, and has grown to be rather a hump than a pack, so that there is no getting rid of it without tearing his whole structure to pieces. In my judgment, as he appears to be sufficiently comfortable under the mouldy accretion, he had better stumble on with it as long as he can. He presents a spectacle which is by no means without its charm for a disinterested and unincumbered observer."

There is all Hawthorne, with his enjoyment of the picturesque, his relish of chiaroscuro, of local colour, of the deposit of time, and his still greater enjoyment of his own dissociation from these things, his "disinterested and unincumbered" condition. His want of incumbrances may seem at times to give him a somewhat naked and attenuated appearance, but on the whole he carries it off very well. I have said that *Our Old Home* contains much of his best writing, and on turning over the book at hazard, I am struck with his frequent felicity of phrase. At every step there is something one would like to quote—something excellently well said. These things are often of the

lighter sort, but Hawthorne's charming diction lingers
in the memory—almost in the ear. I have always
remembered a certain admirable characterisation of
Doctor Johnson, in the account of the writer's visit to
Lichfield—and I will preface it by a paragraph almost
as good, commemorating the charms of the hotel in
that interesting town.

" At any rate I had the great, dull, dingy, and dreary
coffee-room, with its heavy old mahogany chairs and tables,
all to myself, and not a soul to exchange a word with except
the waiter, who, like most of his class in England, had
evidently left his conversational abilities uncultivated. No
former practice of solitary living, nor habits of reticence,
nor well-tested self-dependence for occupation of mind and
amusement, can quite avail, as I now proved, to dissipate the
ponderous gloom of an English coffee-room under such
circumstances as these, with no book at hand save the county
directory, nor any newspaper but a torn local journal of five
days ago. So I buried myself, betimes, in a huge heap of
ancient feathers (there is no other kind of bed in these old
inns), let my head sink into an unsubstantial pillow, and
slept a stifled sleep, compounded of the night-troubles of all
my predecessors in that same unrestful couch. And when I
awoke, the odour of a bygone century was in my nostrils—
a faint, elusive smell, of which I never had any conception
before crossing the Atlantic."

The whole chapter entitled " Lichfield and Uttoxeter "
is a sort of graceful tribute to Samuel Johnson, who
certainly has nowhere else been more tenderly
spoken of.

" Beyond all question I might have had a wiser friend than
he. The atmosphere in which alone he breathed was dense :
his awful dread of death showed how much muddy imperfec-
tion was to be cleansed out of him, before he could be

capable of spiritual existence ; he meddled only with the
surface of life, and never cared to penetrate further than to
ploughshare depth ; his very sense and sagacity were but a
one-eyed clear-sightedness. I laughed at him, sometimes
standing beside his knee. And yet, considering that my native
propensities were toward Fairy Land, and also how much
yeast is generally mixed up with the mental sustenance of a
New Englander, it may not have been altogether amiss, in
those childish and boyish days, to keep pace with this heavy-
footed traveller and feed on the gross diet that he carried in
his knapsack. It is wholesome food even now ! · And then,
how English ! Many of the latent sympathies that enabled
me to enjoy the Old Country so well, and that so readily
amalgamated themselves with the American ideas that seemed
most adverse to them, may have been derived from, or
fostered and kept alive by, the great English moralist. Never
was a descriptive epithet more nicely appropriate than that !
Doctor Johnson's morality was as English an article as a
beef-steak.''

And for mere beauty of expression I cannot forbear
quoting this passage about the days in a fine English
summer :—

" For each day seemed endless, though never wearisome.
As far as your actual experience is concerned, the English
summer day has positively no beginning and no end. When
you awake, at any reasonable hour, the sun is already
shining through the curtains ; you live through unnumbered
hours of Sabbath quietude, with a calm variety of incident
softly etched upon their tranquil lapse ; and at length you
become conscious that it is bedtime again, while there is still
enough daylight in the sky to make the pages of your book
distinctly legible. Night, if there be any such season, hangs
down a transparent veil through which the bygone day
beholds its successor ; or if not quite true of the latitude of
London, it may be soberly affirmed of the more northern
parts of the island that To-morrow is born before its
Yesterday is dead. They exist together in the golden

twilight, where the decrepit old day dimly discerns the face
of the ominous infant ; and you, though a mere mortal, may
simultaneously touch them both, with one finger of recollection and another of prophecy."

The Note-Books, as I have said, deal chiefly with the
superficial aspect of English life, and describe the
material objects with which the author was surrounded.
They often describe them admirably, and the rural
beauty of the country has never been more happily
expressed. But there are inevitably a great many reflections and incidental judgments, characterisations of
people he met, fragments of psychology and social criticism, and it is here that Hawthorne's mixture of subtlety
and simplicity, his interfusion of genius with what I
have ventured to call the provincial quality, is most
apparent. To an American reader this later quality,
which is never grossly manifested, but pervades the
Journals like a vague natural perfume, an odour of
purity and kindness and integrity, must always, for a
reason that I will touch upon, have a considerable
charm ; and such a reader will accordingly take an
even greater satisfaction in the Diaries kept during the
two years Hawthorne spent in Italy ; for in these
volumes the element I speak of is especially striking.
He resigned his consulate at Liverpool towards the close
of 1857—whether because he was weary of his manner
of life there and of the place itself, as may well have
been, or because he wished to anticipate supersession
by the new government (Mr. Buchanan's) which was
just establishing itself at Washington, is not apparent
from the slender sources of information from which
these pages have been compiled. In the month of
January of the following year he betook himself with

his family to the Continent, and, as promptly as possible, made the best of his way to Rome.   He spent the
remainder of the winter and the spring there, and then
went to Florence for the summer and autumn; after
which he returned to Rome and passed a second season.
His Italian Note-Books are very pleasant reading, but
they are of less interest than the others, for his contact
with the life of the country, its people and its manners,
was simply that of the ordinary tourist—which amounts
to saying that it was extremely superficial.   He appears
to have suffered a great deal of discomfort and depression
in Rome, and not to have been on the whole in the best
mood for enjoying the place and its resources.   That he
did, at one time and another, enjoy these things keenly
is proved by his beautiful romance, *Transformation*,
which could never have been written by a man who had
not had many hours of exquisite appreciation of the
lovely land of Italy.   But he took it hard, as it were,
and suffered himself to be painfully discomposed by the
usual accidents of Italian life, as foreigners learn to
know it.   His future was again uncertain, and during
his second winter in Rome he was in danger of losing
his elder daughter by a malady which he speaks of as
a trouble "that pierced to my very vitals."   I may
mention, with regard to this painful episode, that
Franklin Pierce, whose presidential days were over,
and who, like other ex-presidents, was travelling in
Europe, came to Rome at the time, and that the Note-
Books contain some singularly beautiful and touching
allusions to his old friend's gratitude for his sympathy,
and enjoyment of his society.   The sentiment of friendship has on the whole been so much less commemorated
in literature than might have been expected from the

place it is supposed to hold in life, that there is always
something striking in any frank and ardent expression
of it.   It occupied, in so far as Pierce was the object of
it, a large place in Hawthorne's mind, and it is impossible not to feel the manly tenderness of such lines
as these :—

> " I have found him here in Rome, the whole of my early
> friend, and even better than I used to know him ; a heart as
> true and affectionate, a mind much widened and deepened by
> the experience of life.   We hold just the same relation to one
> another as of yore, and we have passed all the turning-off
> places, and may hope to go on together, still the same dear
> friends, as long as we live.   I do not love him one whit the
> less for having been President, nor for having done me the
> greatest good in his power ; a fact that speaks eloquently in
> his favour, and perhaps says a little for myself.   If he had
> been merely a benefactor, perhaps I might not have borne it
> so well ; but each did his best for the other, as friend for
> friend."

The Note-Books are chiefly taken up with descriptions
of the regular sights and "objects of interest," which
we often feel to be rather perfunctory and a little in the
style of the traditional tourist's diary.   They abound in
charming touches, and every reader of *Transformation*
will remember the delightful colouring of the numerous
pages in that novel, which are devoted to the pictorial
aspects of Rome.   But we are unable to rid ourselves of
the impression that Hawthorne was a good deal bored
by the importunity of Italian art, for which his taste,
naturally not keen, had never been cultivated.   Occasionally, indeed, he breaks out into explicit sighs and
groans, and frankly declares that he washes his hands
of it.   Already, in England, he had made the discovery
that he could easily feel overdosed with such things.

"Yesterday," he wrote in 1856, "I went out at about twelve and visited the British Museum ; an exceedingly tiresome affair. It quite crushes a person to see so much at once, and I wandered from hall to hall with a weary and heavy heart, wishing (Heaven forgive me !) that the Elgin marbles and the frieze of the Parthenon were all burnt into lime, and that the granite Egyptian statues were hewn and squared into building stones."

The plastic sense was not strong in Hawthorne ; there can be no better proof of it than his curious aversion to the representation of the nude in sculpture. This aversion was deep-seated ; he constantly returns to it, exclaiming upon the incongruity of modern artists making naked figures. He apparently quite failed to see that nudity is not an incident, or accident, of sculpture, but its very essence and principle ; and his jealousy of undressed images strikes the reader as a strange, vague, long-dormant heritage of his straight-laced Puritan ancestry. Whenever he talks of statues he makes a great point of the smoothness and white-ness of the marble—speaks of the surface of the marble as if it were half the beauty of the image ; and when he discourses of pictures, one feels that the brightness or dinginess of the frame is an essential part of his impression of the work—as he indeed somewhere distinctly affirms. Like a good American, he took more pleasure in the productions of Mr. Thompson and Mr. Brown, Mr. Powers and Mr. Hart, American artists who were plying their trade in Italy, than in the works which adorned the ancient museums of the country. He suffered greatly from the cold, and found little charm in the climate, and during the weeks of winter that followed his arrival in Rome, he sat shivering

M

by his fire and wondering why he had come to such
a land of misery.   Before he left Italy he wrote to his
publisher—"I bitterly detest Rome, and shall rejoice
to bid it farewell for ever; and I fully acquiesce in all
the mischief and ruin that has happened to it, from
Nero's conflagration downward.   In fact, I wish the
very site had been obliterated before I ever saw it."
Hawthorne presents himself to the reader of these
pages as the last of the old-fashioned Americans—and
this is the interest which I just now said that his com-
patriots would find in his very limitations.   I do not
mean by this that there are not still many of his fellow-
countrymen (as there are many natives of every land under
the sun,) who are more susceptible of being irritated than
of being soothed by the influences of the Eternal City.
What I mean is that an American of equal value with
Hawthorne, an American of equal genius, imagination,
and, as our forefathers said, sensibility, would at present inevitably accommodate himself more easily to
the idiosyncrasies of foreign lands.   An American as
cultivated as Hawthorne, is now almost inevitably more
cultivated, and, as a matter of course, more European-
ised in advance, more cosmopolitan.   It is very possible
that in becoming so, he has lost something of his
occidental savour, the quality which excites the good-
will of the American reader of our author's Journals
for the dislocated, depressed, even slightly bewildered
diarist.   Absolutely the last of the earlier race of
Americans Hawthorne was, fortunately, probably far
from being.   But I think of him as the last specimen
of the more primitive type of men of letters; and when
it comes to measuring what he succeeded in being, in
his unadulterated form, against what he failed of being,

the positive side of the image quite extinguishes the
negative. I must be on my guard, however, against
incurring the charge of cherishing a national consciousness as acute as I have ventured to pronounce his own.

Out of his mingled sensations, his pleasure and his
weariness, his discomforts and his reveries, there sprang
another beautiful work. During the summer of 1858, he
hired a picturesque old villa on the hill of Bellosguardo,
near Florence, a curious structure with a crenelated
tower, which, after having in the course of its career
suffered many vicissitudes and played many parts, now
finds its most vivid identity in being pointed out to
strangers as the sometime residence of the celebrated
American romancer. Hawthorne took a fancy to the
place, as well he might, for it is one of the loveliest
spots on earth, and the great view that stretched itself
before him contains every element of beauty. Florence
lay at his feet with her memories and treasures ; the
olive-covered hills bloomed around him, studded with
villas as picturesque as his own ; the Apennines,
perfect in form and colour, disposed themselves opposite, and in the distance, along its fertile valley,
the Arno wandered to Pisa and the sea. Soon after
coming hither he wrote to a friend in a strain of high
satisfaction :—

" It is pleasant to feel at last that I am really away from
America—a satisfaction that I never really enjoyed as long
as I stayed in Liverpool, where it seemed to be that the quint-
essence of nasal and hand-shaking Yankeedom was gradually
' filtered and sublimated through my consulate, on the way
outward and homeward. I first got acquainted with my own
countrymen there. At Rome too it was not much better.
But here in Florence, and in the summer-time, and in this
secluded villa, I have escaped out of all my old tracks, and

M 2

am really remote. I like my present residence immensely.
The house stands on a hill, overlooking Florence, and is big
enough to quarter a regiment, insomuch that each member of
the family, including servants, has a separate suite of
apartments, and there are vast wildernesses of upper rooms
into which we have never yet sent exploring expeditions
At one end of the house there is a moss-grown tower, haunted
by owls and by the ghost of a monk who was confined there
in the thirteenth century, previous to being burnt at the
stake in the principal square of Florence. I hire this villa,
tower and all, at twenty-eight dollars a month ; but I mean
to take it away bodily and clap it-into a romance, which I
have in my head, ready to be written out."

This romance was *Transformation,* which he wrote out
during the following winter in Rome, and re-wrote
during the several months that he spent in England,
chiefly at Leamington, before returning to America.
The Villa Montauto figures, in fact, in this tale as the
castle of Monte-Beni, the patrimonial dwelling of the
hero. " I take some credit to myself," he wrote to the
same friend, on returning to Rome, " for having sternly
shut myself up for an hour or two every day, and come
to close grips with a romance which I have been trying
to tear out of my mind."   And later in the same
winter he says—" I shall go home, I fear, with a heavy
heart, not expecting to be very well contented there.
. . . If I were but a hundred times richer than I am,
how very comfortable I could be ! I consider it a great
piece of good fortune that I have had experience of the
discomforts and miseries of Italy, and did not go
directly home from England. Anything will seem like
a Paradise after a Roman winter." But he got away at
last, late in the spring, carrying his novel with him, and
the book was published, after, as I say, he had worked it

over, mainly during some weeks that he passed at the
little watering-place of Redcar, on the Yorkshire coast,
in February of the following year. It was issued
primarily in England; the American edition immediately followed. It is an odd fact that in the two
countries the book came out under different titles.
The title that the author had bestowed upon it did not
satisfy the English publishers, who requested him to
provide it with another; so that it is only in America
that the work bears the name of *The Marble Faun.*
Hawthorne's choice of this appellation is, by the way,
rather singular, for it completely fails to characterise
the story, the subject of which is the living faun, the
faun of flesh and blood, the unfortunate Donatello.
His marble counterpart is mentioned only in the opening
chapter. On the other hand Hawthorne complained
that *Transformation* " gives one the idea of Harlequin
in a pantomime." Under either name, however, the
book was a great success, and it has probably become
the most popular of Hawthorne's four novels. It is
part of the intellectual equipment of the Anglo-Saxon
visitor to Rome, and is read by every English-speaking
traveller who arrives there, who has been there, or who
expects to go.

It has a great deal of beauty, of interest and grace ;
but it has to my sense a slighter value than its companions, and I am far from regarding it as the masterpiece of the author, a position to which we sometimes
hear it assigned. The subject is admirable, and so are
many of the details ; but the whole thing is less simple
and complete than either of the three tales of American
life, and Hawthorne forfeited a precious advantage in
ceasing to tread his native soil. Half the virtue of

The Scarlet Letter and *The House of the Seven Gables* is
in their local quality ; they are impregnated with the
New England air.   It is very true that Hawthorne had
no pretension to pourtray actualities and to cultivate
that literal exactitude which is now the fashion.   Had
this been the case, he would probably have made a still
graver mistake in transporting the scene of his story to
a country which he knew only superficially.   His tales
all go on more or less "in the vague," as the French
say, and of course the vague may as well be placed in
Tuscany as in Massachusetts.   It may also very well be
urged in Hawthorne's favour here, that in *Transformation* he has attempted to deal with actualities more than
he did in either of his earlier novels.   He has described
the streets and monuments of Rome with a closeness
which forms no part of his reference to those of Boston
and Salem.   But for all this he incurs that penalty of
seeming factitious and unauthoritative, which is always
the result of an artist's attempt to project himself into
an atmosphere in which he has not a transmitted and
inherited property.   An English or a German writer
(I put poets aside) may love Italy well enough, and
know her well enough, to write delightful fictions
about her ; the thing has often been done.   But the
productions in question will, as novels, always have
about them something second-rate and imperfect.
There is in *Transformation* enough beautiful perception of the interesting character of Rome, enough rich
and eloquent expression of it, to save the book, if the
book could be saved ; but the style, what the French call
the *genre*, is an inferior one, and the thing remains a
charming romance with intrinsic weaknesses.

Allowing for this, however, some of the finest pages in

all Hawthorne are to be found in it.   The subject, as I
have said, is a particularly happy one, and there is a great
deal of interest in the simple combination and opposition
of the four actors.   It is noticeable that in spite of the
considerable length of the story, there are no accessory
figures ; Donatello and Miriam, Kenyon and Hilda, exclusively occupy the scene.   This is the more noticeable
as the scene is very large, and the great Roman background is constantly presented to us.   The relations of
these four people are full of that moral picturesqueness
which Hawthorne was always looking for ; he found it in
perfection in the history of Donatello.   As I have said, the
novel is the most popular of his works, and every one
will remember the figure of the simple, joyous, sensuous
young Italian, who is not so much a man as a child, and
not so much a child as a charming, innocent animal, and
how he is brought to self-knowledge and to a miserable
conscious manhood, by the commission of a crime.
Donatello is rather vague and impalpable ; he says too
little in the book, shows himself too little, and falls
short, I think, of being a creation.   But he is enough
of a creation to make us enter into the situation, and
the whole history of his rise, or fall, whichever one
chooses to call it—his tasting of the tree of knowledge
and finding existence complicated with a regret—is
unfolded with a thousand ingenious and exquisite
touches.   Of course, to make the interest complete,
there is a woman in the affair, and Hawthorne has done
few things more beautiful than the picture of the un-
equal complicity of guilt between his immature and
dimly-puzzled hero, with his clinging, unquestioning,
unexacting devotion, and the dark, powerful, more
widely-seeing feminine nature of Miriam.   Deeply

touching is the representation of the manner in which
these two essentially different persons—the woman intelligent, passionate, acquainted with life, and with a
tragic element in her own career ; the youth ignorant,
gentle, unworldly, brightly and harmlessly natural—are
equalised and bound together by their common secret,
which insulates them, morally, from the rest of mankind.   The character of Hilda has always struck me as
an admirable invention—one of those things that mark
the man of genius.   It needed a man of genius and of
Hawthorne's imaginative delicacy, to feel the pro-
priety of such a figure as Hilda's and to perceive the
relief it would both give and borrow.   This pure and
somewhat rigid New England girl, following the voca-
tion of a copyist of pictures in Rome, unacquainted with
evil and untouched by impurity, has been accidentally
the witness, unknown and unsuspected, of the dark deed
by which her friends, Miriam and Donatello, are knit
together.   This is *her* revelation of evil, her loss of perfect innocence.   She has done no wrong, and yet wrong-
doing has become a part of her experience, and she
carries the weight of her detested knowledge upon her
heart.   She carries it a long time, saddened and oppressed
by it, till at last she can bear it no longer.   If I have
called the whole idea of the presence and effect of Hilda
in the story a trait of genius, the purest touch of inspiration is the episode in which the poor girl deposits
her burden.   She has passed the whole lonely summer
in Rome, and one day, at the end of it, finding herself
in St. Peter's, she enters a confessional, strenuous
daughter of the Puritans as she is, and pours out her
dark knowledge into the bosom of the Church—then
comes away with her conscience lightened, not a whit

the less a Puritan than before. If the book contained
nothing else noteworthy but this admirable scene, and
the pages describing the murder committed by Donatello
under Miriam's eyes, and the ecstatic wandering, afterwards, of the guilty couple, through the "blood-stained
streets of Rome," it would still deserve to rank high
among the imaginative productions of our day.

Like all of Hawthorne's things, it contains a great
many light threads of symbolism, which shimmer in the
texture of the tale, but which are apt to break and remain
in our fingers if we attempt to handle them. These
things are part of Hawthorne's very manner—almost,
as one might say, of his vocabulary; they belong much
more to the surface of his work than to its stronger
interest. The fault of *Transformation* is that the element
of the unreal is pushed too far, and that the book is
neither positively of one category nor of another. His
"moonshiny romance," he calls it in a letter; and, in
truth, the lunar element is a little too pervasive. The
action wavers between the streets of Rome, whose literal
features the author perpetually sketches, and a vague
realm of fancy, in which quite a different verisimili-
tude prevails. This is the trouble with Donatello himself. His companions are intended to be real—if they
fail to be so, it is not for want of intention; whereas
he is intended to be real or not, as you please. He is of
a different substance from them; it is as if a painter,
in composing a picture, should try to give you an impression of one of his figures by a strain of music. The idea
of the modern faun was a charming one; but I think it
a pity that the author should not have made him more
definitely modern, without reverting so much to his
mythological properties and antecedents, which are

very gracefully touched upon, but which belong to the
region of picturesque conceits, much more thán to that
of real psychology.   Among the young Italians of to-day
there are still plenty of models for such an image as
Hawthorne appears to have wished to present in the easy
and natural Donatello.   And since I am speaking criti-
cally, I may go on to say that the art of narration, in
Transformation, seems to me more at fault than in the
author's other novels.   The story straggles and wanders,
is dropped and taken up again, and towards the close
lapses into an almost fatal vagueness.

CHAPTER VII.

OF the four last years of Hawthorne's life there is not much to tell that I have not already told. He returned to America in the summer of 1860, and took up his abode in the house he had bought at Concord before going to Europe, and of which his occupancy had as yet been brief. He was to occupy it only four years. I have insisted upon the fact of his being an intense American, and of his looking at all things, during his residence in Europe, from the standpoint of that little clod of western earth which he carried about with him as the good Mohammedan carries the strip of carpet on which he kneels down to face towards Mecca. But it does not appear, nevertheless, that he found himself treading with any great exhilaration the larger section of his native soil upon which, on his return, he disembarked. Indeed, the closing part of his life was a period of dejection, the more acute that it followed directly upon seven years of the happiest opportunities he was to have known. And his European residence had been brightest at the last; he had broken almost completely with those habits of extreme seclusion into which he was to relapse on his return to Concord. " You would be

stricken dumb," he wrote from London, shortly before
leaving it for the last time, " to see how quietly I accept
a whole string of invitations, and, what is more, per-
form my engagements without a murmur. . . . . The
stir of this London life, somehow or other," he adds in
the same letter, "has done me a wonderful deal of good,
and I feel better than for months past. This is strange,
for if I had my choice I should leave undone almost all
the things I do." "When he found himself once more
on the old ground," writes Mr. Lathrop, "with the old
struggle for subsistence staring him in the face again, it
is not difficult to conceive how a certain degree of depression would follow." There is indeed not a little
sadness in the thought of Hawthorne's literary gift,
light, delicate, exquisite, capricious, never too abundant,
being charged with the heavy burden of the maintenance
of a family. We feel that it was not intended for such
grossness, and that in a world ideally constituted he
would have enjoyed a liberal pension, an assured subsistence, and have been able to produce his charming
prose only when the fancy took him.

   The brightness of the outlook at home was not made
greater by the explosion of the Civil War in the spring
of 1861.   These months, and the three years that
followed them, were not a cheerful time for any persons
but army-contractors; but over Hawthorne the war-
cloud appears to have dropped a permanent shadow·
The whole affair was a bitter disappointment to him,
and a fatal blow to that happy faith in the uninter-
ruptedness of American prosperity which I have spoken
of as the religion of the old-fashioned American in
general, and the old-fashioned Democrat in particular.
It was not a propitious time for cultivating the Muse;

when history herself is so hard at work, fiction has
little left to say. To fiction, directly, Hawthorne did
not address himself; he composed first, chiefly during
the year 1862, the chapters of which our *Our Old
Home* was afterwards made up. I have said that,
though this work has less value than his purely imaginative things, the writing is singularly good, and it is
well to remember, to its greater honour, that it was produced at a time when it was painfully hard for a man of
Hawthorne's cast of mind to fix his attention. The air
was full of battle-smoke, and the poet's vision was
not easily clear. Hawthorne was irritated, too, by the
sense of being to a certain extent, politically considered,
in a false position. A large section of the Democratic
party was not in good odour at the North; its loyalty
was not perceived to be of that clear strain which
public opinion required. To this wing of the party
Franklin Pierce had, with reason or without, the credit
of belonging; and our author was conscious of some
sharpness of responsibility in defending the illustrious
friend of whom he had already made himself the advocate. He defended him manfully, without a grain of
concession, and described the ex-President to the public
(and to himself), if not as he was, then as he ought to
be. *Our Old Home* is dedicated to him, and about this
dedication there was some little difficulty. It was represented to Hawthorne that as General Pierce was rather
out of fashion, it might injure the success, and, in plain
terms, the sale of his book. His answer (to his publisher), was much to the point.

"I find that it would be a piece of poltroonery in me to
withdraw either the dedication or the dedicatory letter. My
long and intimate personal relations with Pierce render the

dedication altogether proper, especially as regards this book, which would have had no existence without his kindness ; and if he is so exceedingly unpopular that his name ought to sink the volume, there is so much the more need that an old friend should stand by him.   I cannot, merely on account of pecuniary profit or literary reputation, go back from what I have deliberately felt and thought it right to do ; and if I were to tear out the dedication I should never look at the volume again without remorse and shame.   As for the literary public, it must accept my book precisely as I think fit to give it, or let it alone.   Nevertheless I have no fancy for making myself a martyr when it is honourably and conscientiously possible to avoid it ; and I always measure out heroism very accurately according to the exigencies of the occasion, and should be the last man in the world to throw away a bit of it needlessly.   So I have looked over the concluding paragraph and have amended it in such a way that, while doing what I know to be justice to my friend, it contains not a word that ought to be objectionable to any set of readers.   If the public of the North see fit to ostracise me for this, I can only say that I would gladly sacrifice a thousand or two dollars, rather than retain the good-will of such a herd of dolts and mean-spirited scoundrels."

The dedication was published, the book was eminently successful, and Hawthorne was not ostracised.   The paragraph under discussion stands as follows :—" Only this let me say, that, with the record of your life in my memory, and with a sense of your character in my deeper consciousness, as among the few things that time has left as it found them, I need no assurance that you continue faithful for ever to that grand idea of an irrevocable Union which, as you once told me, was the earliest that your brave father taught you.   For other men there may be a choice of paths—for you but one ; and it rests among my certainties that no man's loyalty is more steadfast, no man's hopes or apprehensions on behalf of our national existence more deeply heartfelt, or more closely intertwined with his possibilities of personal happiness, than those of Franklin Pierce." I know not how well the ex-President liked these lines, but the public thought them admirable, for they served as a kind of formal profession of faith, on the question of the hour, by a loved and honoured writer. That some of his friends thought such a profession needed is apparent from the numerous editorial ejaculations and protests appended to an article describing a visit he had just paid to Washington, which Hawthorne contributed to the *Atlantic Monthly* for July, 1862, and which, singularly enough, has not been reprinted. The article has all the usual merit of such sketches on Hawthorne's part—the merit of delicate, sportive feeling, expressed with consummate grace—but the editor of the periodical appears to have thought that he must give the antidote with the poison, and the paper is accompanied with several little notes disclaiming all sympathy with the writer's political heresies. The heresies strike the reader of to-day as extremely mild, and what excites his emotion, rather, is the questionable taste of the editorial commentary, with which it is strange that Hawthorne should have allowed his article to be encumbered. He had not been an Abolitionist before the War, and that he should not pretend to be one at the eleventh hour, was, for instance, surely a piece of consistency that might have been allowed to pass. " I shall not pretend to be an admirer of old John Brown," he says, in a page worth quoting, " any further than sympathy with Whittier's excellent ballad about him may go; nor did I expect ever to shrink so unutterably from any apophthegm of a sage whose happy lips have uttered a hundred golden sentences "—the allusion here, I suppose, is to Mr. Emerson—" as from that saying (perhaps falsely attributed to so honoured a name), that the death of this blood-stained fanatic has 'made the Gallows as venerable as the Cross!' Nobody was ever more justly hanged. He won his martyrdom fairly, and took it fairly. He himself, I am persuaded (such was his natural integrity), would have acknowledged that Virginia had a right to take the life which he had staked and lost; although it would have been better for her, in the hour that is fast coming, if she could generously have forgotten the criminality of his attempt in its enormous folly. On the other hand, any common-sensible man, looking at the matter unsentimentally, must have felt a certain intellectual satisfaction in seeing him hanged, if it were only in requital of his preposterous miscalculation of possibilities." Now that the heat of that great conflict has passed away, this is a capital expression of the saner estimate, in the United States, of the dauntless and deluded old man who proposed to solve a complex political problem by stirring up a servile insurrection. There is much of the same sound sense, interfused with light, just appreciable irony, in such a passage as the following :—

"I tried to imagine how very disagreeable the presence of a Southern army would be in a sober town of Massachusetts; and the thought considerably lessened my wonder at the cold and shy regards that are cast upon our troops, the gloom, the sullen demeanour, the declared, or scarcely hidden, sympathy with rebellion, which are so frequent here. It is a strange thing in human life that the greatest errors both of

men and women often spring from their sweetest and most
generous qualities ; and so, undoubtedly, thousands of warm-
hearted, generous, and impulsive persons have joined the
Rebels, not from any real zeal for the cause, but because,
between two conflicting loyalties, they chose that which
necessarily lay nearest the heart.   There never existed any
other Government against which treason was so easy, and
could defend itself by such plausible arguments, as against
that of the United States.   The anomaly of two allegiances,
(of which that of the State comes nearest home to a man's
feelings, and includes the altar and the hearth, while the
General Government claims his devotion only to an airy mode
of law, and has no symbol but a flag,) is exceedingly mis-
chievous in this point of view ; for it has converted crowds
of honest people into traitors, who seem to themselves not
merely innocent but patriotic, and who die for a bad cause
with a quiet conscience as if it were the best.   In the vast
extent of our country—too vast by far to be taken into one
small human heart—we inevitably limit to our own State, or
at farthest, to our own little section, that sentiment of
physical love for the soil which renders an Englishman, for
example, so intensely sensitive to the dignity and well-being of
his little island, that one hostile foot, treading anywhere upon
it, would make a bruise on each individual breast.   If a man
loves his own State, therefore, and is content to be ruined
with her, let us shoot him, if we can, but allow him an
honourable burial in the soil he fights for."

To this paragraph a line of deprecation from the
editor is attached ; and indeed from the point of view
of a vigorous prosecution of the war it was doubtless
not particularly pertinent.   But it is interesting as an
example of the way an imaginative man judges current
events—trying to see the other side as well as his own,
to feel what his adversary feels, and present his view
of the case.

But he had other occupations for his imagination

N

than putting himself into the shoes of unappreciative
Southerners. He began at this time two novels, neither
of which he lived to finish, but both of which were published, as fragments, after his death. The shorter of
these fragments, to which he had given the name of *The
Dolliver Romance*, is so very brief that little can be said
of it. The author strikes, with all his usual sweetness,
the opening notes of a story of New England life, and
the few pages which have been given to the world
contain a charming picture of an old man and a child.

The other rough sketch—it is hardly more—is in a
manner complete; it was unfortunately deemed complete enough to be brought out in a magazine as a serial
novel. This was to do it a great wrong, and I do not
go too far in saying that poor Hawthorne would probably not have enjoyed the very bright light that has
been projected upon this essentially crude piece of work.
I am at a loss to know how to speak of *Septimius Felton,
or the Elixir of Life;* I have purposely reserved but a
small space for doing so, for the part of discretion seems
to be to pass it by lightly. I differ therefore widely
from the author's biographer and son-in-law in thinking
it a work of the greatest weight and value, offering
striking analogies with Goethe's *Faust;* and still more
widely from a critic whom Mr. Lathrop quotes, who
regards a certain portion of it as "one of the very
greatest triumphs in all literature." It seems to me
almost cruel to pitch in this exalted key one's estimate
of the rough first draught of a tale in regard to which
the author's premature death operates, virtually, as a
complete renunciation of pretensions. It is plain to any
reader that *Septimius Felton*, as it stands, with its roughness, its gaps, its mere allusiveness and slightness of

treatment, gives us but a very partial measure of
Hawthorne's full intention; and it is equally easy to
believe that this intention was much finer than anything
we find in the book.   Even if we possessed the novel in
its complete form, however, I incline to think that we
should regard it as very much the weakest of Hawthorne's productions.   The idea itself seems a failure,
and the best that might have come of it would have
been very much below *The Scarlet Letter* or *The House
of the Seven Gables*.   The appeal to our interest is not
felicitously made, and the fancy of a potion, to assure
eternity of existence, being made from the flowers which
spring from the grave of a man whom the distiller of
the potion has deprived of life, though it might figure
with advantage in a short story of the pattern of the
Twice-Told Tales, appears too slender to carry the
weight of a novel.   Indeed, this whole matter of elixirs
and potions belongs to the fairy-tale period of taste,
and the idea of a young man enabling himself to live
forever by concocting and imbibing a magic draught,
has the misfortune of not appealing to our sense of
reality or even to our sympathy.   The weakness of
Septimius Felton is that the reader cannot take the hero
seriously—a fact of which there can be no better proof
than the element of the ridiculous which inevitably
mingles itself in the scene in which he entertains his
lady-love with a prophetic sketch of his occupations
during the successive centuries of his earthly immortality.   I suppose the answer to my criticism is that
this is allegorical, symbolic, ideal; but we feel that it
symbolises nothing substantial, and that the truth—
whatever it may be—that it illustrates, is as moonshiny, to use Hawthorne's own expression, as the

allegory itself. Another fault of the story is that a great historical event—the war of the Revolution—is introduced in the first few pages, in order to supply the hero with a pretext for killing the young man from whose grave the flower of immortality is to sprout, and then drops out of the narrative altogether, not even forming a background to the sequel. It seems to me that Hawthorne should either have invented some other occasion for the death of his young officer, or else, having struck the note of the great public agitation which overhung his little group of characters, have been careful to sound it through the rest of his tale. I do wrong, however, to insist upon these things, for I fall thereby into the error of treating the work as if it had been cast into its ultimate form and acknowledged by the author. To avoid this error I shall make no other criticism of details, but content myself with saying that the idea and intention of the book appear, relatively speaking, feeble, and that even had it been finished it would have occupied a very different place in the public esteem from the writer's masterpieces.

The year 1864 brought with it for Hawthorne a sense of weakness and depression from which he had little relief during the four or five months that were left him of life. He had his engagement to produce *The Dolliver Romance*, which had been promised to the subscribers of the *Atlantic Monthly* (it was the first time he had undertaken to publish a work of fiction in monthly parts), but he was unable to write, and his consciousness of an unperformed task weighed upon him, and did little to dissipate his physical inertness. " I have not yet had courage to read the Dolliver proof-sheet," he wrote to his publisher in December, 1863 ;

" but will set about it soon, though with terrible re-
luctance, such as I never felt before. I am most
grateful to you," he went on, "for protecting me from
that visitation of the elephant and his cub. If you
happen to see Mr. ——, of L——, a young man who
was here last summer, pray tell him anything that
your conscience will let you, to induce him to spare me
another visit, which I know he intended. I really am
not well, and cannot be disturbed by strangers, without
more suffering than it is worth while to endure." A
month later he was obliged to ask for a further post-
ponement. " I am not quite up to writing yet, but
shall make an effort as soon as I see any hope of success.
You ought to be thankful that (like most other broken-
down authors) I do not pester you with decrepit pages,
and insist upon your accepting them as full of the old
spirit and vigour. That trouble perhaps still awaits
you, after I shall have reached a further stage of decay.
Seriously, my mind has, for the time, lost its temper
and its fine edge, and I have an instinct that I had
better keep quiet. Perhaps I shall have a new spirit of
vigour if I wait quietly for it; perhaps not." The
winter passed away, but the " new spirit of vigour "
remained absent, and at the end of February he wrote
to Mr. Fields that his novel had simply broken down,
and that he should never finish it. " I hardly know
what to say to the public about this abortive romance,
though I know pretty well what the case will be. I
shall never finish it. Yet it is not quite pleasant for
an author to announce himself, or to be announced, as
finally broken down as to his literary faculty. . . . .
I cannot finish it unless a great change comes over me;
and if I make too great an effort to do so, it will be my

death ; not that I should care much for that, if I could
fight the battle through and win it, thus ending a life
of much smoulder and a scanty fire, in a blaze of glory.
But I should smother myself in mud of my own making.
. . . . I am not low-spirited, nor fanciful, nor freakish,
but look what seem to me realities in the face, and am
ready to take whatever may come. If I could but go to
England now, I think that the sea-voyage and the 'old
Home' might set me all right."

But he was not to go to England ; he started three
months later upon a briefer journey, from which he
never returned. His health was seriously disordered,
and in April, according to a letter from Mrs. Hawthorne, printed by Mr. Fields, he had been "miserably
ill." His feebleness was complete ; he appears to have
had no definite malady, but he was, according to the
common phrase, failing. General Pierce proposed to
him that they should make a little tour together among
the mountains of New Hampshire, and Hawthorne con-
sented, in the hope of getting some profit from the
change of air. The northern New England spring is
not the most genial season in the world, and this was
an indifferent substitute for the resource for which his
wife had, on his behalf, expressed a wish—a visit to
" some island in the Gulf Stream." He was not to go
far ; he only reached a little place called Plymouth, one
of the stations of approach to the beautiful mountain
scenery of New Hampshire, when, on the 18th of May,
1864, death overtook him. His companion, General
Pierce, going into his room in the early morning, found
that he had breathed his last during the night—had
passed away, tranquilly, comfortably, without a sign or
a sound, in his sleep. This happened at the hotel of

the place—a vast white edifice, adjacent to the railway station, and entitled the Pemigiwasset House. He was buried at Concord, and many of the most distinguished men in the country stood by his grave.

He was a beautiful, natural, original genius, and his life had been singularly exempt from worldly preoccupations and vulgar efforts. It had been as pure, as simple, as unsophisticated, as his work. He had lived primarily in his domestic affections, which were of the tenderest kind; and then—without eagerness, without pretension, but with a great deal of quiet devotion—in his charming art. His work will remain; it is too original and exquisite to pass away; among the men of imagination he will always have his niche. No one has had just that vision of life, and no one has had a literary form that more successfully expressed his vision. He was not a moralist, and he was not simply a poet. The moralists are weightier, denser, richer, in a sense; the poets are more purely inconclusive and irresponsible. He combined in a singular degree the spontaneity of the imagination with a haunting care for moral problems. Man's conscience was his theme, but he saw it in the light of a creative fancy which added, out of its own substance, an interest, and, I may almost say, an importance.

THE END.